OPPOSING
VIEWPOINTS®
SERIES

Militias

Other Books of Related Interest:

Opposing Viewpoints Series

Church and State
Democracy
Domestic Violence

Current Controversies Series

Espionage and Intelligence
Government Corruption
The Tea Party Movement

At Issue Series

Guns and Crime
Rebuilding the World Trade Center Site
Should Tasers Be Legal?

> ## "Congress shall make no law ... abridging the freedom of speech, or of the press."

First Amendment to the US Constitution

The basic foundation of our democracy is the First Amendment guarantee of freedom of expression. The Opposing Viewpoints Series is dedicated to the concept of this basic freedom and the idea that it is more important to practice it than to enshrine it.

Militias

Noah Berlatsky, Book Editor

GREENHAVEN PRESS
A part of Gale, Cengage Learning

Detroit • New York • San Francisco • New Haven, Conn • Waterville, Maine • London

GALE
CENGAGE Learning

Elizabeth Des Chenes, *Managing Editor*

© 2012 Greenhaven Press, a part of Gale, Cengage Learning

Gale and Greenhaven Press are registered trademarks used herein under license.

For more information, contact:
Greenhaven Press
27500 Drake Rd.
Farmington Hills, MI 48331-3535
Or you can visit our Internet site at gale.cengage.com.

For product information and technology assistance, contact us at:

Gale Customer Support, 1-800-877-4253.
For permission to use material from this text or product, submit all requests online at www.cengage.com/permissions.

Further permissions questions can be emailed to permissionrequest@cengage.com.

Articles in Greenhaven Press anthologies are often edited for length to meet page requirements. In addition, original titles of these works are changed to clearly present the main thesis and to explicitly indicate the author's opinion. Every effort is made to ensure the Greenhaven Press accurately reflects the original intent of the authors. Every effort has been made to trace the owners of copyrighted material.

Cover Image © Pedro Jorge Henriques Monteiro/Shutterstock.com.

LIBRARY OF CONGRESS CATALOGING-IN-PUBLICATION DATA

Militias / Noah Berlatsky, book editor.
    p. cm. -- (Opposing viewpoints)
    Includes bibliographical references and index.
    ISBN 978-0-7377-5739-2 (hardcover) -- ISBN 978-0-7377-5740-8 (pbk.)
    1. Militia movements--United States. 2. Radicalism--United States.
3. Government, Resistance to--United States. 4. Right-wing extremists--United States. I. Berlatsky, Noah.
    HN90.R3M437 2012
    303.48'4--dc23

    2011034331

Printed in the United States of America
1 2 3 4 5 6 7 16 15 14 13 12

Contents

Chapter 1: Are Militias Dangerous?

Chapter 2: What Groups Are Linked to the Militia Movement?

Chapter 3: How Is the Militia Movement Related to Constitutional Militias?

Chapter 4: What Is the Relationship Between Christianity and Militias?

Why Consider
Opposing Viewpoints?

> "The only way in which a human being
> can make some approach to knowing
> the whole of a subject is by hearing
> what can be said about it by persons of
> every variety of opinion and studying
> all modes in which it can be looked at
> by every character of mind. No wise
> man ever acquired his wisdom in any
> mode but this."
>
> *John Stuart Mill*

In our media-intensive culture it is not difficult to find differing opinions. Thousands of newspapers and magazines and dozens of radio and television talk shows resound with differing points of view. The difficulty lies in deciding which opinion to agree with and which "experts" seem the most credible. The more inundated we become with differing opinions and claims, the more essential it is to hone critical reading and thinking skills to evaluate these ideas. Opposing Viewpoints books address this problem directly by presenting stimulating debates that can be used to enhance and teach these skills. The varied opinions contained in each book examine many different aspects of a single issue. While examining these conveniently edited opposing views, readers can develop critical thinking skills such as the ability to compare and contrast authors' credibility, facts, argumentation styles, use of persuasive techniques, and other stylistic tools. In short, the Opposing Viewpoints Series is an ideal way to attain the higher-level thinking and reading skills so essential in a culture of diverse and contradictory opinions.

In addition to providing a tool for critical thinking, Opposing Viewpoints books challenge readers to question their own strongly held opinions and assumptions. Most people form their opinions on the basis of upbringing, peer pressure, and personal, cultural, or professional bias. By reading carefully balanced opposing views, readers must directly confront new ideas as well as the opinions of those with whom they disagree. This is not to argue simplistically that everyone who reads opposing views will—or should—change his or her opinion. Instead, the series enhances readers' understanding of their own views by encouraging confrontation with opposing ideas. Careful examination of others' views can lead to the readers' understanding of the logical inconsistencies in their own opinions, perspective on why they hold an opinion, and the consideration of the possibility that their opinion requires further evaluation.

Evaluating Other Opinions

To ensure that this type of examination occurs, Opposing Viewpoints books present all types of opinions. Prominent spokespeople on different sides of each issue as well as well-known professionals from many disciplines challenge the reader. An additional goal of the series is to provide a forum for other, less known, or even unpopular viewpoints. The opinion of an ordinary person who has had to make the decision to cut off life support from a terminally ill relative, for example, may be just as valuable and provide just as much insight as a medical ethicist's professional opinion. The editors have two additional purposes in including these less known views. One, the editors encourage readers to respect others' opinions—even when not enhanced by professional credibility. It is only by reading or listening to and objectively evaluating others' ideas that one can determine whether they are worthy of consideration. Two, the inclusion of such viewpoints encourages the important critical thinking skill of objectively evaluating an author's credentials and bias. This evaluation will illuminate an author's reasons for taking a particular stance on an issue and will aid in readers' evaluation of the author's ideas.

It is our hope that these books will give readers a deeper understanding of the issues debated and an appreciation of the complexity of even seemingly simple issues when good and honest people disagree. This awareness is particularly important in a democratic society such as ours in which people enter into public debate to determine the common good. Those with whom one disagrees should not be regarded as enemies but rather as people whose views deserve careful examination and may shed light on one's own.

Thomas Jefferson once said that "difference of opinion leads to inquiry, and inquiry to truth." Jefferson, a broadly educated man, argued that "if a nation expects to be ignorant and free . . . it expects what never was and never will be." As individuals and as a nation, it is imperative that we consider the opinions of others and examine them with skill and discernment. The Opposing Viewpoints Series is intended to help readers achieve this goal.

David L. Bender and Bruno Leone,
Founders

Introduction

"Targeting noncombatants is wrong and cannot be condoned by honorable men. As a soldier, you must die for your war crimes."

> Norman Olson, leader of the
> Northern Michigan Regional
> Militia

On April 19, 1995, a truck bomb exploded in front of the Alfred P. Murrah Federal Building in Oklahoma City. More than 680 people were injured, and 168 were killed. The attackers, Timothy McVeigh and Terry Nichols, were quickly arrested. McVeigh was executed for the crime in 2001; Nichols was sentenced to life imprisonment.

Many have linked McVeigh and Nichols to the militia movement, a loose group of paramilitary organizations that promote civilian defense, express mistrust of the federal government, and are sometimes associated with white supremacist ideology. For example, Lane Crothers in his 2003 book *Rage on the Right: The American Militia Movement From Ruby Ridge to Homeland Security* writes that McVeigh "manifested the values and attitudes of the militia movement enraged." Crothers added that "combining racism with extreme antigovernment paranoia, McVeigh and his fellow conspirators took an action that made sense to them in the context of militia ideology and values." Roger Chapman in his 2010 book *Culture Wars: An Encyclopedia of Issues, Viewpoints, and Voices*, says that McVeigh's "personal ideology was an amalgamation of what he read in comic books, *Soldier of Fortune* magazine, and the writings of the militia movement and Ku Klux Klan."

However, despite these connections, many have pointed out that McVeigh's actual links with the militia movement were tenuous. David B. Kopel in a September 1996 article for *Reason* magazine argues that the only real evidence connecting McVeigh with the militia is the fact that "he and his friend Terry Nichols attended two Militia of Michigan meetings—which, significantly, they were told to leave because they were advocating violence." A 2001 article on the website of the Anti-Defamation League agrees that McVeigh was not "really connected to any particular movement. . . . He never really joined anything, either as a card-carrying member or even as explicit endorsement."

Militia members by and large did not rally behind McVeigh following the bombing. On the contrary, according to Steven M. Chermak in his 2002 book *Searching for a Demon: The Media Construction of the Militia Movement*, "McVeigh hoped to be a martyr; instead militia members despised him because of the negative publicity he brought to the movement."

That negative publicity was intense. Though militia members attempted to distance themselves from McVeigh, the media narrative linking the two of them was extremely damaging. In a June 12, 2001, article on the ABC News website, Bryan Robinson wrote that the Oklahoma City bombing devastated the militia movement. Throughout the '90s, the militia movement was growing, fueled by violent government confrontations at Ruby Ridge, Idaho, in 1992, and at Waco, Texas, in 1993. But, Robinson reported,

> The leveling of the Alfred P. Murrah building, the massive body count, images of bloody children being carried out of the rubble—even the date on which the attack occurred (April 19, the anniversary of end of the siege at Waco)—made everyone involved in a militia look like . . . radical terrorists.

Author Jess Walter noted in a March 30, 2010, roundtable on the *New York Times* website that before the McVeigh bombing, there were 856 active militia organizations. Following the bombing, that number dropped to 200. Historian Catherine

McNol Stock added in the same roundtable that the government's careful handling of the McVeigh case helped to keep him from becoming a martyr and inspiring additional violence. "The federal government worked carefully and deliberately to move [McVeigh's] case through the court system," she said.

While the militia movement went into retreat following the Oklahoma City bombing, it experienced a resurgence in the late 2000s. Even fifteen years later, however, Timothy McVeigh continues to haunt the movement. A February 10, 2011, report on the Michigan television station WWMT Channel 3 profiled the Michigan Militia, the group whose meetings McVeigh had once attended. The members of the group continue to be associated with McVeigh, despite their repeated insistence that he was not one of them. Lee Miracle, a militia member, stated, "'We don't want people who want to hurt Americans. . . . We don't want people who want to hurt babies, we don't want people who want to blow things up because they're mad."

Even when militias explicitly renounce actions like McVeigh's, though, there is concern that they may contribute to violence. Altan Goelman, one of the prosecutors in the McVeigh case, said in a March 31, 2010, interview with Mark Guarino of the *Christian Science Monitor* that militias can inspire those not necessarily closely associated with the movement. According to Goelman, "Anytime you have group-think and this churning of ridiculous ideas back and forth, eventually you'll get someone like McVeigh who's going to say 'I'm going to take the mantle of leadership and fire the shot heard around the world and start the second American revolution.'"

The present volume examines other controversies around the militia movement in chapters titled Are Militias Dangerous? What Groups Are Linked to the Militia Movement? How Is the Militia Movement Related to Constitutional Militias? and What Is the Relationship Between Christianity and Militias? The authors clearly show that questions about militias first raised by the Oklahoma City bombing continue to be hotly debated today.

CHAPTER 1

Are Militias Dangerous?

Chapter Preface

In 2005, Hurricane Katrina flooded much of New Orleans, destroying a large part of the city. In the chaos that followed, some people formed militias in order to prevent looting and maintain order. These militias became a source of some controversy.

In a September 10, 2005, article, the Texas newspaper the *Austin American-Statesman* celebrated a militia formed in the Algiers Point neighborhood of New Orleans as "the ultimate neighborhood watch." The paper reported that after the storm, police and soldiers were otherwise occupied, and the neighborhood was subject to "gangs of intruders." People in the community gathered "a shotgun, pistols, a flare gun, and a Vietnam-era AK-47." They strung empty cans between trees, and when someone stumbled into the cans, they would turn on car headlights and shout warnings to the intruders.

The National Rifle Association (NRA) also praised this action in an October 15, 2007, article on the NRA website. "After Hurricane Katrina, many New Orleans residents legally armed themselves to protect their lives and property from civil disorder. With no way to call for help, and police unable to respond, honest citizens were able to defend themselves and their neighbors against looters, arsonists and other criminals."

Other reporters, however, have argued that the militias formed following Katrina were dangerous and racist. In particular, A.C. Thompson, writing in the *Nation* on January 5, 2009, argued that the Algiers Point militia shot innocent people trying to escape the devastation of Katrina and that they singled out blacks for attack. Thompson says that eleven African Americans were shot in Algiers Point, all by whites. Thompson reports that one man, Donnell Herrington, was walking with two companions when without warning he was shot in the neck with a shotgun. The assailants were three white men who shouted at him as he fled, "Get him! Get that n－－－!"

Thompson argues:

Facing an influx of refugees, the residents of Algiers Point could have pulled together food, water and medical supplies for the flood victims. Instead, a group of white residents, convinced that crime would arrive with the human exodus, sought to seal off the area, blocking the roads in and out of the neighborhood by dragging lumber and downed trees into the streets. They stockpiled handguns, assault rifles, shotguns and at least one Uzi and began patrolling the streets in pickup trucks and SUVs. The newly formed militia, a loose band of about fifteen to thirty residents, most of them men, all of them white, was looking for thieves, outlaws or, as one member put it, anyone who simply "didn't belong."

The following chapter's viewpoints further explore the question of whether militias help to protect law-abiding citizens or whether they encourage dangerous violence.

> *"There still exist a growing number of extremists who are already armed and preparing for potential conflict with the government."*

The Militia Movement Is Dangerous

Abraham H. Foxman

Abraham H. Foxman is national director of the Anti-Defamation League and author of The Deadliest Lies: The Israel Lobby and the Myth of Jewish Control. *In the following viewpoint, he argues that right-wing extremism was responsible for the 1995 Oklahoma City bombing. He says that extremism has experienced a resurgence, epitomized by conspiracy theories and militia movements. Foxman concludes that the government must be vigilant in defending against violent right-wing extremism.*

As you read, consider the following questions:

1. According to Foxman, what are "The Turner Diaries"?
2. What does the author say may have inspired the resurgence in right-wing extremism?
3. Many militia members and right-wing extremists believe that the passage of health care reform will be followed by what, according to Foxman?

Fifteen years ago, on April 19, 1995, Timothy McVeigh exploded a truck bomb in front of the Murrah Federal Building in Oklahoma City. The explosion killed 168 men, women and children, and wounded hundreds more.

Homegrown Terrorism

The bombing shocked the nation—and was a powerful reminder that homegrown terrorism could be just as brutal and hateful as terrorism spawned on foreign shores.

Prior to the bombing, a few watchdog organizations had issued warnings about the dangerous growth of right-wing extremist groups, including the then-new militia movement. In 1994 the Anti-Defamation League issued a report titled, "Armed and Dangerous: Militias Take Aim at the Federal Government" which turned out, unfortunately, to be extremely prescient.

But it took the bombing itself to make most Americans aware of the seriousness of the threat and the potentially violent nature of these groups and their individual members.

McVeigh and his accomplice, Terry Nichols, had an intense hatred of the government stoked by conspiracy theories of government plots to kill the Branch Davidians during their 1993 standoff with the government. Their actions were further inspired by "The Turner Diaries," a fictional blueprint for a white revolution by former neo-Nazi leader William Pierce.

McVeigh and Nichols were hardly alone. From 1995 into the early 2000s, hundreds of anti-government extremists and white supremacists were convicted for a variety of plots, conspiracies and violent acts.

Over the years, though, other serious crises emerged, including the 9/11 terrorist attacks, the wars in Afghanistan and Iraq, the ongoing threat of another attack by Al Qaeda, and a rise in domestic and international Muslim extremism.

The lessons of Oklahoma City, though not forgotten, somehow seemed less urgent in the new millennium.

Concerns About the Militia Movement Are Justified

The militia movement is the youngest of the major right-wing anti-government movements in the United States ... yet it has seared itself into the American consciousness as virtually no other fringe movement has. The publicity given to militia groups in the wake of the Oklahoma City bombing in 1995, when the militia movement was erroneously linked to that tragedy, made them into a household name. Indeed, reporters, pundits and politicians alike have used the term so frequently that it is often tossed about carelessly as a synonym for virtually any right-wing extremist group.

Yet the militia movement is neither generic nor dismissible as a comic subject. If militia groups were not, in fact, involved with the Oklahoma City bombing, they have nevertheless embroiled themselves since 1994 in a variety of other bombing plots, conspiracies and serious violations of law. Their extreme anti-government ideology, along with their elaborate conspiracy theories and fascination with weaponry and paramilitary organization, lead many members of militia groups to act out in ways that justify the concerns expressed about them by public officials, law enforcement and the general public.

Anti-Defamation League, "The Militia Movement," 2005. www.adl.org

Those lessons may be more important today [April 2010] than they have been in many years. Over the last 18 months, motivated by factors ranging from the recession to the election [in 2008] of Barack Obama [a nonwhite man] as president, the extreme right in the United States has undergone a startling resurgence.

Resurgence of the Militia Movement

Anti-government movements such as the militia and the sovereign citizen movements have increased greatly in size and activity. The militia movement alone has quadrupled in size over the past two years, with more than 200 active anti-government militia groups. White supremacist movements, though not experiencing the same increase in size, have demonstrated greatly increased levels of agitation, including calls for violence.

Over the past year, right-wing extremists made headlines through violent acts and plots, including a fatal shooting at the U.S. Holocaust Memorial Museum in Washington, D.C., the deadly ambush of three police officers in Pittsburgh, and the gunning down of a physician in his own church in Kansas, among others.

The arrest of nine members of the anti-government Hutaree Militia, accused of a plot to kill law enforcement officers and their families to create a confrontation with the government that would spark a broader uprising, was just the most recent example of an extremist militia group making headlines.

For experts who monitor the extreme right, the parallels between today and 1995 are disturbing. Extremists have revived the anti-government conspiracy theories that motivated many plots in the 1990s, ranging from alleged "concentration camps" constructed by the Federal Emergency Management Agency to the imminent suspension of the Constitution and imposition of martial law.

Even the Hutaree Militia had ties to militia propagandist Mark "Mark from Michigan" Koernke, the "patriot" leader made infamous during the Oklahoma City investigation after being mistakenly linked to the bombing.

The anti-government sentiments of the Hutaree Militia are unfortunately shared by a growing number of domestic extremists, both within and outside the militia movement. The Hutaree arrests are important, but there still exist a growing number of extremists who are already armed and preparing for potential conflict with the government.

Monitoring of Internet chatter related to health care reform [passed in March 2010] and other recent issues indicates that many militia members and anti-government extremists believe this legislation will be followed by the mass legalization of illegal immigrants, postponement or elimination of democratic elections, martial law and gun confiscation. Like the Hutaree, they believe that a "New World Order" of tyrannical rule is coming.

As we remember the victims of the Oklahoma City bombing 15 years ago, and vow that we will never again allow domestic terrorists to strike on our soil, it is essential that our society and law enforcement remain cognizant of the ever-present danger of right-wing extremism in the United States.

Law enforcement agencies should be prepared to apprehend extremists who cross the line from protected speech to illegal actions. Community leaders and elected officials should take this renewed threat of domestic extremism seriously.

The most fitting way to honor the victims of Oklahoma City, and to make sure that their sacrifices were not in vain, is to ensure that no new McVeigh is able to emerge from the shadows to wreak destruction and sorrow.

> *"The belief in [militias'] imminent war with the government . . . is 'greatly exaggerated.'"*

The Danger Posed by Militias Is Exaggerated

Todd A. Heywood

Todd A. Heywood writes for the Michigan Messenger *and is the Michigan Capitol correspondent for the publication* Between the Lines. *In the following viewpoint, he reports on the Southeast Michigan Volunteer Militia and notes that the group is not committed to armed conflict with the government, even though some seem to subscribe in part to some antigovernment conspiracy theories. He concludes by discussing a social scientist's opinion that the danger from most militias is exaggerated.*

As you read, consider the following questions:

1. Who is Matt Savino and why, according to Heywood, has he received so much media attention?
2. How did Jeff Kindy's journey to the militia begin, according to Heywood?
3. According to Amy Cooter, as cited by the author, what is

the difference between most militias and fringe groups like the Hutaree?

Four miles down a long, winding paved road from the guard house at Island Lake Recreation Area in Brighton [Michigan] is a rustic camping area surrounded by trees and marsh. Down the road are "rustic cabins." The area is marked with signs indicating it is a no shooting area. On Saturday morning, the Mill Pond was being fished, and dozens of bicyclists circled the park's paved road.

Southeast Michigan Volunteer Militia

In the campground sat a group of about two dozen folks. Some are gathered around a picnic table, strategically placed beside a screen tent with cooking gear and a posted yellow sign that says "Warning: Men Cooking." Some are whittling at another picnic table across the raised metal fire pit. The spirit is jovial—but for the camouflage gear and holstered side arms, one would think they had wandered into a family camping weekend.

Meet the Southeast Michigan Volunteer Militia [SMVM], which spent the day in training exercises at the Island Lake park.

Michigan Messenger joined the group for its monthly training Saturday at the invitation of the group's coordinator, Lee Miracle. Miracle, a pudgy man with a graying goatee and black hair, works for the post office. He is joined by his wife and three kids. Also joining the SMVM this weekend were members of the Lenawee County Militia, headed up by Matt Savino, and the Lansing Area Militia.

A photographer from Reuters [news service] hovers around the group, snapping pictures. A reporter from the Washington, D.C., office of National Public Radio breezes in, interviews Miracle and leaves as the rain starts falling. The Reuters photographer soon follows.

During the rest of the day, the group studies the creation of snares and other things to capture wild game. Others from the group study rudimentary compass and mapping techniques. They learn how to measure paces, and run a simple compass course. And late in the morning, a small group sets out on a pre-planned nine mile hike.

Lunch consists of cold cuts on white bread.

Perceptions of Extremism Remain

Miracle wanted *Messenger* to visit to see what the militia was really about. This is not the militia of the 1995 Oklahoma City Bombing lore, he says; the paranoia is gone, and these are decent citizens just working on survival skills, including weapons training. They are not convinced of an imminent war with the government, or a nebulous New World Order, he insists.

And they are certainly not the Hutaree, the Adrian [Mich.]-based Christian militia rounded up in raids the previous weekend and indicted in federal court on charges of plotting to kill police officers and foment a war against the government.

Miracle, and the group's spokesman, Michael Lackomar, encourage conversations with any of the group's members. Lackomar jokes that he is pleased to see Savino present, taking the focus off him. Savino has been receiving a great deal of media attention not only as the militia in Michigan's only Muslim member, but also as the man a Hutaree fugitive reached out to for help while running from the feds.

Savino rebuffed those requests from Joshua Stone, the son of the Hutaree leader, during the March 27 [2010] raids of the Hutaree properties, and later attempted to assist the FBI in arresting the fugitive.

Extremism Remains

The rosy view of militias that Miracle gives is in stark contrast to some other militia leaders around the country, many of whom speak of a coming war between the militias and the government as inevitable. Indeed, the FBI says that is what the Hutaree were attempting to trigger with their alleged plot to kill police officers and blow up their funerals—and at least one prominent militia leader has said that they nearly succeeded.

Mike Vanderboegh, a 57 year old Alabama militia leader raised in Michigan, said that militias all over the country went on high alert when the Hutaree were raided and were prepared to take up arms against the government if there had been any bloodshed during the raids or if another Waco or Ruby Ridge–type situation developed.[1] As more facts about the raids came out, he said, the militias slowly stood down.

But he still wrote on his blog, "This could have been one hell of a lot worse than it was. Today we avoided the beginning of a civil war. I do not know how long we will be able to do that in the future, given Fed cowboy clumsiness, but the fact that we were the ones who did not take counsel of our fears—and who [to quote the New Testament] 'put away childish things' and did not overreact—bodes well at least for ensuring that we don't lose the moral high ground when the Feds, finally, in frustration at our refusal to submit to their diktats [orders], open fire on us. After that, it will be an open source insurgency using Fourth Generation Warfare. And we WILL win."

That kind of messaging—an imminent war with the feds— has soaked the mythos surrounding the modern militia movement since the early 1990s. It was solidified when Timothy McVeigh and Terry Nichols blew up the Alfred P. Murrah Federal Building in Oklahoma City on April 19, 1995. From that point on, the media presented the militia movement, which is a fragmented collection of loosely affiliated groups, as a monolithic movement that was overwhelmingly paranoid, bent on war with the government and largely inhabited by neo-Nazis and other racialists.

Those perceptions continue today and the *Messenger* wanted to find out from militia members directly how they felt about the government, about the inevitability of a war with the government and about the kinds of government conspiracies that are frequently mentioned by other right wing extremist groups.

Conspiracy Theories

We selected several members of the SMVM to speak with. They included Tom Jr., a 24-year Marine reservist from Canton; his father, Tom Sr., an unemployed 48-year-old also from Canton; and Jeff Kindy, 42-year-old from Wyandotte. All three rejected out of hand the ideology of end-time Christianity, and rejected racism.

Kindy's journey to the militia began with a power blackout in 2003 that left people in Michigan, Ohio, New York and other states without power, some for as many as four days. Kindy said he was caught unprepared.

"I was caught off guard. We didn't have water, we didn't have extra food. We weren't really ready for it and that kinda really woke me up. So I keep a pantry now," Kindy said. "It's all about preparedness."

For him, the militia is a place to learn those skills to be prepared for any event—whether it's an act of terrorism, an invasion, or a natural disaster. For him, the militia has been characterized, unfairly, as "a bunch of crazies running through the woods with guns," and he says that is neither accurate or fair.

"In fact, we usually get from the media, 'well when are you going to run through the woods with your guns?' That's not at all what we do. Like today we're doing primitive snares, traps, dead falls, stuff to use in a survival type situation if perhaps power goes out, or there is an ice storm, or something happens in a disaster where the transportation can't get through and refill the shelves in the grocery store, so there is some way for us to procure food for our family and friends," he says.

Kindy says he comes from a "military family." He met his wife while in the reserves in Jackson, where he served for five years. He served three years on active duty as well.

"I looked at signing back up for the military service but my physical attributes and my age and the fact I've got three kids prevented me from doing so. So I wanted to serve my country and protect our Constitution and our rights so I looked at other venues. And found the militia was probably the closest thing I could get involved with more on a civilian aspect," Kindy said. "My son wants to join the army but he is legally blind so he can't. So we looked at the militia together and decided that that was the best deal for us to get involved and protect the Constitution and what not and learn survival skills and different things like that."

Both Tom Jr. and Tom Sr. also hail from military backgrounds. Tom Jr. served a tour in Iraq as a marine, and is currently in the reserves. His father was also active duty military.

For Tom Sr., his time in the military taught him to respect guns. For Tom Jr., it supported his love of his country. Both men said the militia helped connect them to those feelings.

And while the militia has long been painted as preparing for an inevitable war with the government, all three men said that was not their goal—nor did they necessarily think such a conflict was inevitable.

Kindy was the least convinced of the three about the rise of a New World Order, or NWO, which is a phrase indicating an oppressive one world government.

The Hutaree militia believed that police and federal agents were part of the New World Order, and thus their enemies.

"I can see some of the stuff that the conspiracy theorists are coming up with. And I don't see it all [in the militias]. Still I am really not sure where I stand on that. It's not something that I focus on," Kindy said. "I am more interested in focusing on government regulations in my local area and being a part of that. And then selecting the right people from my area to represent me into the bigger government and so forth."

"To me the NWO is the U.N., the banks, the old Noblesse Oblige philosophy of kings and queens, basically the meaning of which is that basically the common man is incapable of governing himself so it is the duty of the elite to do it," said Tom Jr. "Which, if you think about it from one perspective is a noble philosophy—to sacrifice your life in service to the people to govern them. But the problem with that is that the people need to govern themselves, one, and two, such a philosophy inevitably leading towards corruption and tyranny. Which inevitably leads towards rebellion and violence."

Not the Tea Party

But Tom Jr. offers a caveat. "Is it theoretically possible (that there will be a conflict with the government)? Sure. If such a thing were to happen, the only thing I can say about that, I can say without any doubt, with all certainty—the one thing I would never do is fire upon military personnel, law enforcement or civilians."

He believes if there was such a war it would result from foreign troops coming into the U.S., something he says the U.S. military is a "barrier" to.

For Tom Sr., his views on the New World Order and the coming conflict are similarly non-committal.

"I mean it's possible," he says as he is packing up his camping gear. "It seems like it's going that way. There seems to be some kind of effort. A sort of a consolidation of power. And I can see why that would be. Tyranny always repeats itself."

But he says the Constitution is such an important document for him, and other patriots, because it foresaw the rise of tyranny, and allowed for the citizens to stop it.

Asked specifically if he thinks conflict between the militias and the government is inevitable, he is emphatic in his response.

"No. No. No," he says. "If it happens to be, then I am a soldier against it. If it happens not to be, then I am still a soldier."

All three men talked about a discomfort with big government, saying that the federal government was overstepping its bounds. Kindy talked about federal gun regulations, which he said he could agree with in part. Tom Jr. talked about the health care legislation.

But don't mistake them for the Tea Party movement.

"The tea parties are basically, in my opinion, people fed up with overtaxation," Kindy said. "And that is why they are using the example of the original tea party. You know we're fed up with being overtaxed. They do kind of go hand in hand, but not really. They are more like cousins, not brothers."

"The Tea Party movement was not a Republican thing. It was never supposed to be a Republican thing, or a Democrat thing. The Tea Party movement was a group of people who really just want to step away from the two party system," says Tom Jr., who said he was disappointed with the movement. "And then the Republicans hijacked it because they want to maintain the status quo. They want to stay where they're at. They don't want to be taken away from their position."

But there is a darker distrust of the government these men harbor.

One of the popular memes among patriot and militia groups is a belief that the government is preparing FEMA [Federal Emergency Management Agency] internment camps in which to put Americans. And while none of the three militia members we spoke to would take a bold position either way, they indicated a great deal of suspicion based on fragmentary beliefs.

"I can't say (if the camps are for relocation or not)—again without showing some conspiracy theories and sensationalism about it; I can't say what their motivation is," says Tom Jr. "But look at the facts. They've been building camps. What they've been building them for—well, whatever they say they have been building them for, is it true or not? I don't know. Again. There's no way to know. There's this overwhelming air of fear that the government is perpetuating. If they really cared they would do something to quell those fears. They would do something and show a little transparency in their actions."

"I've heard it. I've seen the videos on YouTube," Kindy says. "I have seen pictures of the plastic coffins. And it's disturbing but there's no documentation of what they're for. I don't know if you are going to find documentation saying this is for the mass graves we're going to instill."

Most Militias Are Not the Extreme

Amy Cooter, University of Michigan, Ph.D. Candidate: You know, the vast majority of this [militia] movement aren't so antagonistic toward the government that they're ready to start a fight. I think what we've seen with [the Hutaree] that's been in the news these last few days is sort of the extreme of this movement.

Most of the militia movements see their involvement as more of a political protest than anything. They do practice. They do target practice and general training with firearms. But for the most part, they're not particularly afraid of the government and aren't worried about them banging down their door and coming after their individual rights.

[CNN anchor Ali] Velshi: So in this fight that may happen between them and the government, where do the rest of us fall? Is this a fight? Do they imagine it to be a war? Or is it a "we're armed, and don't—don't interfere in our lives"?

Cooter: You know, for the most part, like I said, most of these groups don't see this war as coming. For those that do, I think that they see themselves as a last line of defense for their communities. They don't see the average, everyday citizen as being on the side of the federal government or as being a target of their activity, for the most part.

CNN.com, March 30, 2010. http:// transcripts.cnn.com.

"There are some bills that were pushed through. But I don't think they were FEMA camp bills. They were bills to protect the government," says Tom Sr. "I think they are fearful something could happen. There's a lot of stress out there. I think they're really fearful and they are protecting themselves. I think if anything, this country becomes a FEMA camp."

Tom Sr. believes the U.S. government can easily shut down the country, creating swaths of controlled areas, in which it can shut off water, food, electricity, etc., thus gaining control of the region in the event of a conflict or wide scale civil disturbance.

"I am very frustrated and angry with the government. But the reason I am here isn't because I am angry or frustrated with the government," said Tom Jr. "Am I scared of it? Am I concerned about it? Am I sometimes angry and frustrated about it? Yes. I am here to exercise and protect my Constitutional rights. Simple as that. Not to attack the government, or to prepare for an attack from the government. You know. It's simple and pure; just my Constitutional rights."

Paranoia Is Exaggerated

Amy Cooter, a PhD candidate at [the] U[niversity] of M[ichigan] in sociology, is finishing up a thesis about the militia movement in the state. She has spent countless hours with the various Michigan militias but not, interestingly, with the Hutaree. She said when she first began her research, she was told by nearly everyone else in the militia movement not to spend time with the Hutaree because they were reckless, extreme and unsafe.

She says the belief in imminent war with the government, while advocated by some leaders like Vanderboegh, is "greatly exaggerated."

Emphasizing a variety of views among the different militias, Cooter told the *Messenger*, "Fringe groups like Hutaree have a strong religious element; most groups do not. Most modern groups are not racist, at the group level. Many feel that conflict with the government is inevitable, but it takes the form more of legislative fights over the 2nd Amendment, and not a take-up-arms-and-fight approach."

"Most of them do not want conflict," she said. "Many are combat veterans and say they don't want to see anything like that in their country, let alone their neighborhoods. They see it as a last resort if someone is literally banging down their door, and will use other means to accomplish their ends first (voting, contacting Congress, etc.—which they regularly do)."

And contrary to the Hutaree, who allegedly looked to kill police officers, Cooter said, "I've spent two years getting to know these groups very well, have seen them have working relationships with law enforcement agencies, and few of them buy into these kinds of polarizing views."

Note

1. Waco, Texas, and Ruby Ridge, Idaho, were sites of extremist group activity that was violently quashed by government forces in 1993 and 1992, respectively.

35

> *"The fact that the president is an African American has injected a strong racial element into . . . parts of the radical right, like the militias."*

The Militia Movement Has Become Racist

Larry Keller

Larry Keller writes for the Southern Poverty Law Center, a civil rights group that focuses on race and hate issues. In the following viewpoint, he says that militia activity has risen since 2008. He links this resurgence to the economic downturn, the election of a black president, and concerns over immigration. The last two factors, he says, have made the new militia movement more explicitly racist than the movement was in the 1990s. Keller adds that the militia movement has committed significant acts of violence and that more such acts are likely.

As you read, consider the following questions:

1. According to Keller, what are so-called sovereign citizens?
2. Who are Oath Keepers, according to the author?
3. What conspiracy theories does Keller say that the

anti-immigrant movement has brought to the militia movement?

Almost 10 years after [the end of the 1990s] it seemed to disappear from American life, there are unmistakable signs of a revival of what in the 1990s was commonly called the militia movement. From Idaho to New Jersey and Michigan to Florida, men in khaki and camouflage are back in the woods, gathering to practice the paramilitary skills they believe will be needed to fend off the socialistic troops of the "New World Order."

A Black President and Immigration

One big difference from the militia movement of the 1990s is that the face of the federal government—the enemy that almost all parts of the extreme right see as the primary threat to freedom—is now black. And the fact that the president is an African American has injected a strong racial element into even those parts of the radical right, like the militias, that in the past were not primarily motivated by race hate. Contributing to the racial animus have been fears on the far right about the consequences of Latino immigration.

Militia rhetoric is being heard widely once more, often from a second generation of ideologues, and conspiracy theories are being energetically revived or invented anew. "Paper terrorism"— the use of property liens, bogus legal documents and "citizens' grand juries" to attack enemies and, sometimes, reap illegal fortunes—is again proliferating, to the point where the government has set up special efforts to rein in so-called "tax defiers" and to track threats against judges. What's more, patriot fears about the government are being amplified by a loud new group of ostensibly mainstream media commentators and politicians.

It's not 1996 all over again, or 1997 or 1998. Although there has been a remarkable rash of domestic terrorist incidents since [Barack] Obama's election in November [2008], it has not reached the level of criminal violence, attempted terrorist attacks and white-hot language that marked the militia movement at its peak. But militia training events, huge numbers of which are now viewable on YouTube videos, are spreading. One federal agency estimates that 50 new militia training groups have sprung up in less than two years. Sales of guns and ammunition have skyrocketed amid fears of new gun control laws, much as they did in the 1990s.

The situation has many authorities worried. Militiamen, white supremacists, anti-Semites, nativists, tax protesters and a range of other activists of the radical right are cross-pollinating and may even be coalescing. In the words of a February [2009] report from law enforcement officials in Missouri, a variety of factors have combined recently to create "a lush environment for militia activity."

"You're seeing the bubbling [of antigovernment sentiment] right now," says Bart McEntire, who has infiltrated racist hate groups and now is the supervisory special agent for the U.S. Bureau of Alcohol, Tobacco, Firearms and Explosives in Roanoke, Va. "You see people buying into what they're saying. It's primed to grow. The only thing you don't have to set it on fire is a Waco or Ruby Ridge."[1]

Another federal law enforcement official knowledgeable about militia groups agrees. He asked not to be identified because he is not authorized to speak publicly about them. "They're not at the level we saw in '94–'95," he says. "But this is the most significant growth we've seen in 10 to 12 years. All it's lacking is a spark. I think it's only a matter of time before you see threats and violence."

Racism and Anti-Semitism

In fact, threats and violence from the radical right already are accelerating. . . . In recent months, men with antigovernment, racist, anti-Semitic or pro-militia views have allegedly committed a series of high-profile murders—including the killings of six law enforcement officers since April [2009].

Most of these recent murders and plots seem to have been at least partially prompted by Obama's election. One man "very upset" with the election of America's first black president was building a radioactive "dirty bomb"; another, a Marine, was planning to assassinate Obama, as were two racist skinheads in Tennessee; still another angry at the election and said to be interested in joining a militia killed two sheriff's deputies in Florida. A man in Pittsburgh who feared Jews and gun confiscations murdered three police officers. Near Boston, a white man angered by the alleged "genocide" of his race shot to death two African immigrants and intended to murder as many Jews as possible. An 88-year-old neo-Nazi killed a guard at the Holocaust Museum in Washington, D.C. And an abortion physician in Kansas was murdered by a man steeped in the ideology of the "sovereign citizens" movement.

So-called sovereign citizens are people who subscribe to an ideology, originated by the anti-Semitic Posse Comitatus of the 1980s, that claims that whites are a higher kind of citizen—subject only to "common law," not the dictates of the government—while blacks are mere "14th Amendment citizens" who must obey their government masters. Although not all sovereigns subscribe to or even know about the theory's racist basis, most contend that they do not have to pay taxes, are not subject to most laws, and are not citizens of the United States.

Authorities and anecdotal evidence suggest that sovereign citizens—who, along with tax protesters and militia members, form the larger Patriot movement—may make up the most dramatically reenergized sector of the radical right. In February [2009], the FBI launched a national operation targeting white supremacists and "militia/sovereign citizen extremist groups" after noting an upsurge in such organizations, the *Wall Street Journal* reported. The aim is to gather intelligence about "this emerging threat," according to an FBI memo cited by the newspaper.

Increasingly, sovereign citizens are claiming they aren't subject to income taxes—so much so that the Department of Justice [in 2008] kicked off a National Tax Defier Initiative to deal with the volume of cases. At the same time, more and more seem to be engaging in "paper terrorism," even though more than 30 states passed or strengthened laws outlawing the filing of unjustified property liens and simulating legal process (by setting up pseudo-legal "common law courts" and "citizens' grand juries") in response to sovereign activity in the 1990s.

A Michigan man whose company allegedly doubled as the headquarters of a militia group, for example, was arrested in May on charges that he placed bogus liens on property owned by courthouse officials and police officers to harass them and ruin their credit. In March [2009], authorities raided a Las Vegas printing firm where meetings of the "Sovereign People's Court for the United States" were conducted in a mock courtroom. Seminars allegedly were taught there on how to use phony documents and other illegal means to pay off creditors. Four people were arrested on money-laundering, tax and weapons charges.

Due to a spike in "inappropriate communications," including many from sovereign citizens, the U.S. Marshals Service has opened a clearinghouse in suburban Washington, D.C., for assessing risks to court personnel. The incidents include telephone and written threats against federal judges and prosecutors, as well as bomb threats and biochemical incidents. In fiscal 2008, there were 1,278 threats and harassing communications—more than double the number of six years earlier. The number of such incidents is on pace to increase again in fiscal 2009. Sovereign citizens account for a small percentage of the cases, but theirs are more complex and generally require more resources, says Michael Prout, assistant director of judicial security for the marshals. "They are resourceful groups," he adds.

Some sovereign citizen attempts to skirt the law have been farcical. An Arkansas jury needed only seven minutes in April to convict Richard Bauer, 70, of robbing a bank. Bauer had argued that the government took his money several times, leaving him with almost nothing. "I'm a constitutionalist," he insisted, adding that "every single act was justifiable." A month earlier, a Pennsylvania man charged with drunken driving told court officials that they lacked jurisdiction over him because he was a "sovereign man." Then he changed his mind and pleaded guilty. In Nevada, a sovereign citizen—perhaps a [children's author] Dr. Seuss fan—used the peculiar punctuation of names that is favored by the movement; his name, he declared, was "I am: Sam."

But few of the cases are that amusing. In February, a New York man who once declared himself a "sovereign citizen" of the "Republic of New York" and said that he enjoyed studying "the organic Constitution and the Bill of Rights" allegedly shot and killed four people. His murder case was pending at press time.

Swearing at the Government

Oath Keepers, the military and police organization that was formed earlier this year [2009] and held its April muster on Lexington Green [in Lexington, Massachusetts, where the American Revolution purportedly began], may be a particularly worrisome example of the Patriot revival. Members vow to fulfill the oaths to the Constitution that they swore while in the military or law enforcement. "Our oath is to the Constitution, not to the politicians, and we will not obey unconstitutional (and thus illegal) and immoral orders," the group says. Oath Keepers lists 10 orders its members won't obey, including two that reference U.S. concentration camps.

That same pugnacious attitude was on display after conservatives attacked an April report from the U.S. Department of Homeland Security (DHS) that suggested a resurgence of radical right-wing activity was under way. "We will not fear our government; they will fear us," one man, who appeared to be on active duty in the Army, said in an angry video sent to the Oath Keepers blog. In another video at the site, a man who said he was a former Army paratrooper in Afghanistan and Iraq described President Obama as "an enemy of the state," adding, "I would rather die than be a slave to my government." The Oath Keepers site soon began hawking T-shirts with slogans like "I'm a Right Wing Extremist and Damn Proud of It!"

In April [2009], Oath Keepers founder Stewart Rhodes—a Yale Law School graduate and former aide to U.S. Rep. Ron Paul (a Texas Republican and hard-line libertarian)—worried about a coming dictatorship. "We know that if the day should come where a full-blown dictatorship would come, or tyranny . . . it can only happen if those men, our brothers in arms, go along and comply with unconstitutional, unlawful orders," Rhodes told conspiracy-minded radio host Alex Jones. "Imagine if we focus on the police and military. Game over for the New World Order."

He's not the first to think so. In the 1990s, retired Phoenix cop and conspiracy enthusiast Jack McLamb created an outfit called Police Against the New World Order and produced a 75-page document entitled *Operation Vampire Killer 2000: American Police Action Plan for Stopping World Government Rule.*

It's not known how large Oath Keepers is. But there is some evidence beyond the group's mere existence to suggest that to-day's Patriots are again making inroads into law enforcement—the leak of the DHS report, along with those of a couple of similar law enforcement reports, was likely the work of a sworn officer. Rhodes claims to know a federal officer leaked the DHS report, and says Oath Keepers is "hearing from more and more federal officers *all the time.*"

The group does seem to be on the radar of federal law en-forcement officers. In May [2009], a member complained on the group's website of a visit to his farm by FBI agents who asked him, he said, about training he provides in firearms, survival skills and the like.

One Oath Keeper is longtime militia hero Richard Mack, a former sheriff of a rural Arizona county who collaborated with white supremacist Randy Weaver on a book and who, along with others, won a U.S. Supreme Court decision that weakened the Brady Bill gun control law in the 1990s. "The greatest threat we face today is not terrorists; it is our federal government," Mack says on his website. "One of the best and easiest solutions is to depend on local officials, especially the sheriff, to stand against federal intervention and federal criminality."

Mack's views echo those of the Posse Comitatus, which believed that sheriffs are the highest law enforcement authorities in America. "I pray for the day that a sheriff in this country will arrest an IRS [Internal Revenue Service] agent for trespassing or attempting to victimize citizens in that particular sheriff's county," Mack said in a video he made for Oath Keepers.

Waco and Ruby Ridge

Why are militias and the larger Patriot movement making a comeback?

The original militia movement took off in the mid-1990s, with the first large militias appearing in 1994 and growth continuing over the next several years. The movement reflected widespread anger over what was seen as the meddling of a relatively liberal administration in Washington—from gun control to environmental laws to a variety of other federal mandates. But what really ignited the movement was the bloodshed in Ruby Ridge, Idaho, and Waco, Texas. In 1992, during a standoff between white supremacist Randy Weaver's family in Idaho and federal agents—a confrontation that began with Weaver's sale of an illegal weapon—Weaver's son and wife were killed, along with a U.S. marshal. The following year, some 80 members of the gun-loving Branch Davidian cult died in a fire that ended a 52-day standoff with federal agents in Texas. Thousands of Americans saw these events as proof that the federal government was prepared to murder its own citizens in order to enforce a kind of liberal orthodoxy—a so-called "New World Order" (NWO) that reflected the economic and political globalization that militia backers felt was robbing their country of its independence and unique culture.

The movement was animated by a welter of conspiracy theories, the bulk of them decrying NWO plots that were said to be aimed at imposing socialism on the United States, sending patriotic Americans to prison camps, destroying farmers with secret weather machines, and so on. Most militia enthusiasts also blamed the 1995 Oklahoma City bombing on the government— it was a "false flag" operation carried out by the [Bill] Clinton Administration, they contended, and designed to soften up the American public to accept draconian anti-terrorism legislation.

But the movement of the '90s ultimately wound down, almost petering out after the turn of the millennium. That was for a variety of reasons, including the arrests of many militia backers in terrorist plots, the jailing of hundreds of others on weapons violations, and the violence the movement continued to produce even after 168 people, including 19 children, were murdered in Oklahoma City by men steeped in the ideology of both militias and racist hate groups. The failure of any of the many dire Patriot predictions or conspiracy theories to come true also hurt the movement, as did the 2000 election of a conservative president, which had the effect of defusing militia backers' anger. Apocalyptic warnings from militia leaders about an expected "Y2K" collapse on Jan. 1, 2000, also turned out to be entirely without merit, becoming a kind of final nail in the coffin of the movement.

Why the Return?

Now, it seems, they are back. Every month, there are militia trainings announced around the country—and untold numbers that are not publicized. The Internet teems with training videos, information about meetings and rallies, far-fetched rumors and conspiracy theories. Joining 1990s militia stalwarts like [Ted] Gunderson and Mack is a new generation of activists, as exemplified in the case of Edward Koernke. Koernke's father, Mark Koernke, was a prominent '90s militia propagandist known as "Mark from Michigan." The elder Koernke served nearly six years in prison on charges that included assaulting police. Today, his son hosts an Internet radio show devoted to all things militia.

Militias and Racism in Post-Katrina New Orleans

The way Donnell Herrington tells it, there was no warning. One second he was trudging through the heat. The next he was lying prostrate on the pavement, his life spilling out of a hole in his throat, his body racked with pain, his vision blurred and distorted.

It was September 1, 2005, some three days after Hurricane Katrina crashed into New Orleans, and somebody had just blasted Herrington, who is African-American, with a shotgun. "I just hit the ground. I didn't even know what happened," recalls Herrington. . . .

The attack occurred in Algiers Point. . . .

When the hurricane descended on Louisiana, Algiers Point got off relatively easy. While wide swaths of New Orleans were deluged, the levees ringing Algiers Point withstood the Mississippi's surging currents, preventing flooding; most homes and businesses in the area survived intact. As word spread that the area was dry, desperate people began heading toward the west bank, some walking over bridges, others traveling by boat. . . .

Facing an influx of refugees, the residents of Algiers Point . . . sought to seal off the area, blocking the roads in and out of the neighborhood by dragging lumber and downed trees into the streets. They stockpiled handguns, assault rifles, shotguns and at least one Uzi and began patrolling the streets in pickup trucks and SUVs. The newly formed militia, a loose band of about fifteen to thirty residents, most of them men, all of them white, was looking for thieves, outlaws or, as one member put it, anyone who simply "didn't belong."

A.C. Thompson, The Nation, January 5, 2009.

The current resurgence has several apparent causes. In the largest sense, it is again a response to real societal stresses and strains, from the seemingly inevitable rise of multiculturalism to the faltering economy to another liberal administration, this one headed by a black man. Similar factors have driven the number of race-based hate groups, as distinct from Patriot groups, from 602 in 2000 to 926 in 2008, according to research by the Southern Poverty Law Center.

"This frequently happens when elections favor the political left and the society is seen as moving toward greater social equality or away from traditional societal hierarchies," Chip Berlet, a long-time analyst of the radical right at Political Research Associates, said in a June newsletter. "In this scenario, it is easier for right-wing demagogues to successfully demonize liberals," immigrants and others.

In fact, the anti-immigration movement is both fueling and helping to racialize the antigovernment Patriot resurgence. More and more, members of nativist groups like the Minutemen are adopting core militia ideas and fears. And they have contributed their own conspiracy theories—about the secret Mexican "Plan de Aztlan" to reconquer the American Southwest, and another involving the secretly arranged merger of the United States, Mexico and Canada into a "North American Union"—to the long list of nefarious plots already identified by the Patriot movement.

Far-right fears of conspiracies have come from other quarters, as well, most notably from the so-called "birthers" who have filed a series of lawsuits making the claim that Obama is not a U.S. citizen. These spurious claims first gained traction when prominent extremists like writer Jerome Corsi, politician Alan Keyes and Watergate felon and radio show host G. Gordon Liddy questioned the validity of the president's birth certificate. Many Patriots have also adopted conspiracy theories about secret government involvement in events like the Sept. 11, 2001, terrorist attacks and the crash of TWA Flight 800 in 1996.

"The current political environment is awash with seemingly absurd but nonetheless influential conspiracy theories, hyperbolic claims and demonized targets," Berlet concluded. "And this creates a milieu where violence is a likely outcome."

Note

1. In 1993 the federal government raided an extremist compound in Waco, Texas, killing seventy-six people. Ruby Ridge was the site of a violent confrontation between government agents and extremists in Idaho in 1992.

> *"The left, with the media's obvious help,
> is bound and determined to turn
> [the right-wing militias'] political
> disagreement into something about
> race and hate."*

The Militia Movement's Racism Is a Leftist Fabrication

Bruce McQuain

Bruce McQuain is a retired infantry officer with twenty-eight years' service who blogs regularly at QandO.net on politics and BlackFive .net on military affairs. In the following viewpoint, he argues that there is no evidence of a racist militia backlash against President Barack Obama. He says hate-group rhetoric has not increased and that it is as marginal as ever on the right. He says that accusations of racism and of increased militia activity have been created by the left to unfairly tar those with legitimate policy differences on the right.

As you read, consider the following questions:

1. According to McQuain, what incident involving the New Black Panthers should the Southern Poverty Law Center have been involved in investigating?

2. What does the author say caused the rise of the militia movement in the 1990s?

3. What is Camp Vigilance, and why does McQuain argue it is not linked to a recent rise in militia violence?

I've watched the Southern Poverty Law Center's [SPLC] rise over the years as the self-proclaimed expert on "extremist hate groups." But what I've also deduced over those years, mostly by observing when and what we hear from them, is it is primarily an organization that sees the "right-wing" as the primary threat to America.

Exaggerated Threats

They'd most likely deny that and point to their "Hate Groups Map" and its inclusion of black separatist organizations, but they even put a caveat on their inclusion of them:

> Although the Southern Poverty Law Center recognizes that much black racism in America is, at least in part, a response to centuries of white racism, it believes racism must be exposed in all its forms. White groups espousing beliefs similar to Black Separatists would be considered clearly racist. The same criterion should be applied to all groups regardless of their color.

Other than a mention of what the organization is, i.e. Nation of Islam or New Black Panther party, and a short description of their beliefs, you'll not find much on the SPLC's website about what would be considered "leftist extremist" hate groups.

And you'll find nothing in their legal docket where they've ever taken one of these groups on in court. One would think the voter intimidation by two New Black Panthers in Philadelphia that occurred in the last [2008] presidential election would be right in their sweet spot, but there is no indication whatsoever that such activity even caught their attention.

So it stands to reason that the SPLC loves it when a Democratic administration comes into being because it naturally plays into their primary focus and that elevates their importance (because gullible media outlets will naturally buy into what they're selling) and we see the "rise of the right-wing militias" nonsense begin again.

Today's featured gullible media outlet is ABC News, which breathlessly repeats, er, reports that, yup, those right-wing militias, they're rising again:

> Experts who track hate groups across the U.S. are growing increasingly concerned over violent rhetoric targeted at President Obama, especially as the debate over health care intensifies and a pattern of threats emerges.

Any guess as to what "experts" they're talking about?

And you have to love the examples ABC News uses to transition into tarring the right as a bunch of racists:

> The Secret Service is investigating a Maryland man who held a sign reading "Death to Obama" and "Death to Michelle and her two stupid kids" outside a town hall meeting this week. And in New Hampshire, another man stood across the street from a Presidential town hall with his gun on full display.
>
> Los Angeles police officers apprehended a man Thursday after a standoff with him inside a red Volkswagen Bug car in Westwood, CA—the latest disturbing case *even though officials said the man had mental problems.*

Ya think? Tell me, thinking back, did John Hinckley represent the "extremist left" when he shot [conservative president] Ronald Reagan [in 1981]? I don't believe that question was ever raised by the SPLC at the time.

We have a guy legally carrying a gun (although admittedly doing so at an inappropriate time and at an inappropriate place) and one sign among thousands which is inappropriate all included with one mentally whacked individual in [California] and we're ready to conclude that right-wing hate-mongers—violent right-wing hate-mongers (or "evil-mongers" if you're a [Democratic Senate majority leader] Harry Reid fan)—are on the rise.

All About Obama

There's another bit of "mongering" going on here—fearmongering.

> "I don't think these are simply people who are mentally ill or off their rocker," Mark Potok, director of the Intelligence Project at the Southern Poverty Law Center, told ABC News of those behind the threats. "In a very real sense they represent a genuine reaction, a genuine backlash against Obama."

Notice the substance of the SPLC's accusation. He's speaking of townhall protesters in general and essentially saying while the three in question may actually include one real whack job, they represent the true feelings of the protesters—this is all about Obama.

And the inference of making it "all about Obama"? Say it with me now—he's a black man. And that, dear reader, makes it all about racism.

If you don't believe that's what they're suggesting, you might want to read their website. From the short description of their "special report" on "The Return of the Militias":

> After virtually disappearing from public view a decade ago, the antigovernment militia movement is surging across the country—*fueled by fears of a black president*, the changing demographics of the country and fringe conspiracy theories increasingly spread by mainstream figures.

Anyone remember why the militia movement began back then [in the 1990s]? Well it had nothing to do with a "black president" and everything to do with what appeared to be an expansion of government to include another health care grab.

From the first article in the "special report," two things to note. One, it's all anonymous "reports":

> Authorities around the country are reporting a worrying up-tick in Patriot activities and propaganda. "This is the most significant growth we've seen in 10 to 12 years," says one. "All it's lacking is a spark. I think it's only a matter of time before you see threats and violence."

Frankly this is akin to National Enquirer [a gossip tabloid] reporting. . . .

Two, it is all about Obama being a "black man."

> *A key difference this time is that the federal government—the entity that almost the entire radical right views as its primary enemy—is headed by a black man.* That, coupled with high levels of non-white immigration and a decline in the percentage of whites overall in America, has helped to racialize the Patriot movement, which in the past was not primarily motivated by race hate.

Nothing to support this at all, simply an assertion that fits the agenda of those writing the "special report." Who is spreading fear now?

No Evidence of Racism

The second "report" of the SLPC's "special report" by Larry Keller:

> One big difference from the militia movement of the 1990s is that the face of the federal government—the enemy that almost all parts of the extreme right see as the primary threat to freedom—is now black. . . .

Sound familiar? Yup, it doesn't take a literary critic to understand that Larry wrote not only his own screed [personal opinion], but the first unattributed screed as well. So essentially, what we have to this point is Larry Keller's opinion, unsourced and undocumented, as to what is going on.

What's pitiful is in the 4 paragraphs leading up to the paragraph above, he gives not one scintilla of support for the premise he lays out there—it's all about Obama because he's black. The people he's talking about haven't been mentioned in any news reports as being attendees at a single townhall protest that I've seen. But that doesn't stop him from inferring that they're the primary movers in this protest movement. . . .

And you have to love this:

> At the Jacksonville, Fla., July [2009] tea party, some protesters carried signs that compared President Obama to Adolf Hitler.

Gasp! I'll bet Keller was all over the "[President George W.] Bush/Hitler" comparisons for the last 8 years, wasn't he? Uh, no. . . .

The last of the "special reports" is by David Holthouse. It's all about "Camp Vigilance," a Minute Man community in San Diego. You're left with the impression that this boiling, seething, ready-to-explode community has arisen rather recently and is representative of the growing threat. You're certainly left to assume it has arisen since the recent presidential election. And you're also left to extrapolate this one place as typical of all those now protesting (why is never clear).

It was, however, established in 2006, well within the Bush administration and, apparently, despite Mr. Holthouse's attempt to make this new and fresh, it seems it's the same collection of whack jobs that have been out there pushing conspiracy theories about the Illuminati and global bankers since I've been alive. It should also be noted that up to now, they've apparently done nothing at Camp Vigilance to bring law enforcement down on them.

The point of all this is the left, with the media's obvious help, is bound and determined to turn this political disagreement into something about race and hate.

"I think the president has, in effect, triggered fears amongst fairly large numbers of white people in this country that they are somehow losing their country, that the battle is lost," Potok told ABC News. "The nation that their Christian white forefathers created has somehow been taken from them."

Yup—without "fairly large numbers of white people" available to blame this twisted message on, Potok and SPLC are out of a job, aren't they?

> "I can't help but be grateful that
> the federal government does have
> the power to keep surveillance on
> extremists of all kinds."

The Government Is Right to Monitor the Threat Posed by Some Militias

Eileen Pollack

Eileen Pollack is a writer of fiction, short stories, creative nonfiction, articles, and reviews. In the following viewpoint, she argues that while many militia members are not dangerous, there are some like the radical Christian Hutaree who pose a real threat. She notes that militia activity exists around her home in Michigan and that her son was acquainted with one of the children of the Hutaree. She concludes that it is important for government to monitor extremists and to arrest and prosecute those like the Hutaree who pose a real threat.

As you read, consider the following questions:

1. What does Pollack say that the emphasis of 2010's Tax Blast seemed to be?

2. According to the author, who might it be dangerous for

her son to argue with and why?

3. Who is Mark Koernke, and why was he arrested, according to Pollack?

Afew weeks ago [in spring of 2010], after nine members of the Hutaree militia were arrested in and around Ann Arbor, [Michigan,] an editor at the [*New York*] *Times* asked me to follow up my series on the election by writing an op-ed piece about militia activities in Michigan. He wanted to know if the average person living in the state had any contact with the militia. Coincidentally, just a few days earlier, my son Noah, who was home from college, informed me that he'd gone to school with the son of a couple that belonged not only to the militia, but to the Hutaree. I worked frantically to research and write an essay for *The Times*; as usual, they chopped it up and cut it by 2/3. But I was happy to see it finally run in the April 19th edition of the paper, on the same page as an essay by [former US president] Bill Clinton about his memories of the Oklahoma City bombing [in 1995 by right-wing extremist Timothy McVeigh]. . . .

Militia Field Day

Here's the original essay, as I wrote it . . .

The flags flapping above the picnic area warned "Liberty or Death" and "Do Not Tread on Me," while the man behind the registration table sold bull's-eyes and IRS 1040 forms to be used as targets for the adult and youth shooting contests later in the day. But most of the action at last Saturday's "Militia Field Day aka Tax Blast: Open Carry Family Picnic & Tea Party," held at Island Lake Recreation Area in Brighton, Michigan, consisted of militia members and their families chowing down on pulled pork and kielbasa [polish sausage]. One militia man squatted beneath a tree, giving lessons on how to start a fire using two sticks. Another played "Dixie" on his harmonica. A tiny girl in pink clutched a stuffed dinosaur with one hand and her father with the other; like most of the militia members, he wore army boots, fatigues, and a big black pistol on his hip.

Tax Blast is an annual event. But this year [2010], the emphasis seemed less on riddling 1040 forms with bullets than demonstrating that the Southeast Michigan Volunteer Militia [SMVM] is in no way affiliated with the Hutarees, an apocalyptic Christian branch of the militia, nine of whose members recently were arrested for allegedly plotting to assassinate police officers and kill any nonmilitia members who stumbled upon their reconnaissance operations in the woods.

Living in Ann Arbor, I don't usually feel threatened by the militias. Most members are just indulging their fantasies of being warriors without having to sign up for the army and go to Afghanistan or Iraq. They want to be heroes and save their neighbors from disaster. Many of the guys in the yuppie southeast Michigan branch of the militia consider themselves to be socially progressive libertarians and welcome anyone, Jewish, black, or Muslim, who declares him- or herself willing to defend Michigan from invasion, whether by the federal government or foreign terrorists. (The lid on one chafing dish at the picnic read "Kosher Meals Available," while another dish proclaimed its contents to be suitable for vegans and vegetarians. The kosher dish stood empty until an exceedingly large armed man wearing a black T-shirt that read "When I Snap You'll Be the First To Go" filled the tinfoil tray with Hebrew National hot dogs.) I even understand some militia members' fears: I don't like wiretaps or surveillance cameras, and, during the [George W.] Bush administration, I often found myself frightened of my own government.

But I am chilled to think of thousands of armed militia members from all over the country marching on Washington, D.C., and Virginia this coming Monday to "celebrate" the fifteenth anniversary of the Oklahoma City bombing and "restore the Constitution." "PATRIOTS WILL ASSEMBLE IN VIRGINIA AND MARCH ON WASHINGTON ON APRIL 19. THIS WILL BE AN 'OPEN CARRY' MARCH. BRING YOUR

GUNS. PATRIOTS WILL TAKE BACK AMERICA FROM THE [BARACK] OBAMA OCCUPATIONAL GOVERNMENT," reads a post to a [right-wing radio talk show host] Rush Limbaugh fan site on Google. "Civil war starts April 19, 2010? Nervous nation waits for armed march on Washington, DC (bang)" proclaims the website of a group called New World Order Fighters.

Good Militias and Bad Militias

Many of the militia members at the Tax Blast told me they can't take time off from their jobs to travel to Washington for the protest. But a rifle team leader named Solo, an IT [information technology] specialist who lives in Troy, plans on attending. He worries that President Obama is going to make an end run around the Second Amendment by requiring every bullet in America to be inscribed with a traceable serial number, or by pricing ammo out of the reach of the common citizen, or by allowing [secretary of state] Hillary Clinton to negotiate an international treaty that [binds] us to the same anti-gun laws that European nations must obey. "I want to let people on the east and west coasts know that people in the middle of the country want to keep their guns," Solo told me. The timing of the event—April 19—doesn't bother him; what bothers him is that "that asshole" Timothy McVeigh "ruined a perfectly good holiday."

Solo and most of the other militia members who intend to march on Washington aren't planning on killing anyone. But I can't help but wonder how can we distinguish those who are from those who aren't? If I come upon a group of people dressed in fatigues, toting weapons, and ranting about the New World Order, how am I supposed to tell whether they belong to a slightly paranoid libertarian division of the militia, or a violently delusional, racist, homophobic, anti-Semitic branch?

A few months before the Hutarees were arrested, the supervisor of a town not far from Ann Arbor called upon two brigades of the Michigan Militia, including the Hutarees, to help find two missing residents. When this story came to light, my son saw a

© 2010 John Cole, *The Scranton Times-Tribune*, and PolitcalCartoons.com.

photo of one of the Hutarees and said, "Hey, I know her." As it turned out, the woman's stepson was my son's high school classmate, and my son, who considers himself a socialist, sometimes engaged the boy in friendly discussions of their opposing political beliefs. The boy's stepmother and father live in Manchester, a town I visit to browse for antiques, attend the chicken broil, and enjoy ice cream at the Dairy Queen beside the river, although the woman apparently joined the Hutarees after meeting several members at a Ron Paul rally right here in Ann Arbor.

My son also knows the militia member who coordinated the search, having interviewed the man for an article he wrote for his school newspaper describing an event at which several hundred 9/11 Truthers gathered at the University of Michigan to publicize their theory that the destruction of the World Trade Center was an inside job. I admire my son for engaging people so unlike himself in political discussions. But I hate to think of him getting in an argument with a rightwing extremist who is packing a weapon and believes that socialists are destroying our country and, as I heard on a podcast describing the reasons for the upcoming march, "the only way we can stop them is to make them stop."

The Crazies Are Still Out There

Any group that sees a reason to "celebrate" the anniversary of the Oklahoma City bombing terrifies me. I moved to Michigan eight months before Timothy McVeigh blew up the Murrah Building. Although McVeigh wasn't a member of the Michigan Militia, he did attend one of their meetings and practiced building bombs at a farm 120 miles northeast of Ann Arbor. At the time, Mark Koernke, aka "Mark from Michigan, the Voice of the Militia," worked as a janitor at the U[niversity] of M[ichigan], where I teach, and in his off hours hosted a vitriolic radio show, which he used as a forum to support McVeigh's incendiary views. The radio show was broadcast from Koernke's hometown of Dexter, a quaint village a few miles up the river from Ann Arbor, where my then-husband and I would take our son to buy cider and homemade donuts.

After the carnage in Oklahoma City and President Clinton's exit from the White House [in 2000], much of the militia activity in Michigan subsided. Koernke got sent to jail for fleeing the scene of a robbery he didn't commit and resisting the efforts of police to question him. But the crazies still were out there. One afternoon in 2003, I was reading a book about a virulently racist and anti-Semitic hate group called the Christian Identity movement when I received a call from Zingerman's Deli asking me to come downtown to finalize plans for my son's bar mitzvah. I got in my car and, a few blocks from the restaurant, noticed Christian Identity bumper stickers on the truck in front of me.

Then came the 2008 presidential campaign [won by Barack Obama] and the near collapse of the American economy, and the militias regained support, not only in towns to the north and west, but in the southeast corner of the state, around Ann Arbor and Detroit. The SMVM was quick to distance itself from the Hutarees; their spokesperson even hinted to me at the Tax Blast that he and his guys had a hand in alerting the FBI to the Hutarees' agenda. But the anger and paranoia that fueled the resurgence of the militias didn't evaporate overnight because a few extremists were arrested. Not long after the FBI took the Hutarees into custody, I tuned my laptop to the Intelligence Report, once again being broadcast from Dexter by Mark Koernke, who had served his sentence and was treating his listeners to the ominous click of a bullet being loaded in the chamber of a gun and warnings about his perimeter being secured and the first nine people who breached that perimeter being doomed.

Libertarian militia members might welcome non-Christian members, but when I read on the Hutarees' website that they were prepared to use the sword "to defend all those who belong to Christ and save those who aren't," I wonder what they intended to "save" me and my Jewish and Muslim neighbors from. So, despite my desire to preserve the liberties granted by our Constitution, I can't help but be grateful that the federal government does have the power to keep surveillance on extremists of all kinds and seems able to figure out which few members of which few militias are serious about wanting to assassinate police officers or shoot people like me who might wander into the woods while they are training for Armageddon.

> "[The government's and media's attitude toward militias] exaggerates the threats at hand."

The Government Has Overstated the Militia Threat

Jesse Walker

Jesse Walker is the managing editor of Reason Magazine, *a libertarian publication of news and commentary. In the following viewpoint, he argues that the government case against the Hutaree militia is weak, since it may have just been engaging in extreme speech rather than actually conspiring to kill police officers. Suggestions that the Hutaree are part of a rising tide of right-wing violence are also overstated, he says. He argues that the Hutaree are despised by most militias and by others on the right. He concludes that conflating the Hutaree with other right-wing groups is un-American and will lead to the curtailment of free speech.*

As you read, consider the following questions:

1. What kind of speech did the judge in the Hutaree case say was deserving of protection, according to Walker?
2. On what grounds does the author argue that the Oath Keepers and the John Birchers are not likely to plot violence like the Hutaree?

3. What is a Brown Scare, according to Walker?

Flash back to the end of March [2010], when the authorities hauled in nine members of the Hutaree, a Christian paramilitary group, and charged them with plotting a mass assassination of police officers. The media quickly added the arrests to the ongoing narrative of "rising right-wing violence," with the Michigan-based militants cast as the leading edge of a smoldering paramilitary threat. Newscasters and columnists touted a report by the Southern Poverty Law Center (SPLC) claiming that the number of anti-government "Patriot" organizations is skyrocketing. An "astonishing 363 new Patriot groups appeared in 2009," the center declared, "with the totals going from 149 groups (including 42 militias) to 512 (127 of them militias)— a 244% jump." If you worry about political violence, the SPLC warned, such growth "is cause for grave concern."

Hutaree Case Is Falling Apart

A month later, the Hutaree case is in a state of flux, with prosecutors appealing Judge Victoria Roberts' ruling that the accused should be released on bond while awaiting their trial. There are signs that the judge is unimpressed with the state's case, and she has stressed that prosecutors must demonstrate that the arrestees were guilty of an actual conspiracy to kill cops, not just loose talk. Even "hate-filled, venomous speech," she said, is "a right that deserves First Amendment protection."

Obviously we don't know what evidence has yet to be introduced at trial. Perhaps there really is more at issue here than some chest-beating chatter; perhaps there's a good reason to think a genuine murder plot was underway. But either way, we've learned enough about the Hutaree in the last month to know that the media narrative that greeted their arrests hasn't held up. Assume the worst-case scenario: that the defendants really were planning a massacre and that they really were capable of carrying it out. They still aren't the vanguard of the right-wing revolution. The Hutaree are isolated and despised, not just by the American mainstream but by the bulk of the groups on the SPLC's Patriot list. Indeed, the government may have had the help of some anti-Hutaree militiamen as it forged its case against the accused.

That much-cited Southern Poverty Law Center list lumps together a very varied set of organizations, blurring the boundary between people who might have sympathy for Hutaree-style plots and people who would want no part of them. "Generally," the SPLC explains, the groups on its roster "define themselves as opposed to the 'New World Order,' engage in groundless conspiracy theorizing, or advocate or adhere to extreme antigovernment doctrines." That covers a lot of ground. Using this list to track the threat of right-wing terrorism is like tracking the threat of jihadist terrorism by counting the country's mosques.

The SPLC acknowledges that not all the groups on its list "advocate or engage in violence or other criminal activities." But its spokespeople regularly suggest that there's a slippery slope at work. The ubiquitous Mark Potok, for example, has told the *Las Vegas Review-Journal* that he wouldn't accuse any member of the Oath Keepers, a group whose chapters take up 53 spots on the watch list, "of being [Oklahoma City bomber] Timothy McVeigh." But the organization is spreading paranoia, he continued, and "these kinds of conspiracy theories are what drive a small number of people to criminal violence."

There Is No Slippery Slope

This is a variation on the long-discredited gateway drug argument, in which the fact that people who abuse heroin are likely to have tried pot first is seen as evidence that pot causes heroin abuse. Potok is also understating the different directions that people in Patriot circles can be pulled. The Oath Keepers have distanced themselves from violent-minded supporters, and the whole point of the organization is to persuade the government's agents to refuse orders the group considers unconstitutional, a central tactic not of terrorism but of nonviolent civil resistance. Meanwhile, 41 groups on the SPLC list are chapters of the John Birch Society. Far from an adjunct to the militias, the Birchers—notorious for their own conspiracy theories—devoted a lot of effort in the '90s to debunking the more elaborate conspiracy yarns popular in much of the militia world. They frown on insurrectionary violence, too, sometimes suggesting that it merely plays into the hands of the Grand Cabal.

The militia subculture itself is far from united. The University of Hartford historian Robert Churchill—author of an excellent book on the militias, *To Shake Their Guns in the Tyrant's Face*—has identified two distinct though sometimes overlapping elements within the movement: the "constitutionalists" and the "millenarians." While the first group stresses civil liberties and organizes in public, the second segment is more prone to paranoid, violent, and apocalyptic rhetoric and is more likely to form secret cells. The Hutaree hail from the far end of the millenarian side of the spectrum. There doesn't seem to be any love lost between them and the area's dominant militia, the constitutionalist Southeast Michigan Volunteer Militia (SMVM), which greeted the March arrests by denouncing the Hutaree as a religious cult. Mike Lackomar of the SMVM even told *The Detroit News* that the Hutaree had called his militia asking for assistance during the raids and had been rebuffed.

Skeptical readers may object that this is exactly what you'd expect an organization to do if its erstwhile allies are facing federal charges. (The anti-militia writer David Neiwert, for example, greeted the news by declaring that Lackomar's group was "throwing the Hutaree folks under the bus.") But we have independent confirmation of the tensions between the SMVM and the Hutaree. Amy Cooter, a doctoral candidate in sociology at the University of Michigan, has been doing fieldwork in the state's militia movement for two years now. She first heard of the Hutaree long before the arrests, when members of the

SMVM told her a "story about some crazy people who came to train with them once"; the visitors handled themselves unsafely and were "told not to come back." Cooter also notes that the SMVM, a secular group that includes a convert to Islam, distrusted the "strong anti-Muslim sentiment" it detected in the Hutaree. The SMVM did "keep the lines of communication open," she notes, "but that was to keep an eye on them as much as anything else."

What did "keep an eye on them" mean? In mid-April both Lackomar and Lee Miracle—a member of yet another group, the Southeast Michigan Militia—told *The Detroit News* that they had warned the Federal Bureau of Investigation about the Hutaree over a year ago. Miracle says he urged the agency to check out the Hutaree website, telling his contact, "See if they creep you out the way they creep me out." Another member reportedly infiltrated the Hutaree and is now serving as a cooperating witness in the case. The FBI would neither confirm nor deny these claims. But Cooter backs up a portion of the militiamen's account, telling the *News* that she had seen emails about the Hutaree that militia members sent to the Bureau.

None of this is unprecedented. Back in the 1990s, several would-be terrorists in the Patriot milieu were arrested after other militiamen got wind of their plans and alerted police.

Focus on Crimes, Not Ideas

Some writers have suggested that the Hutaree arrests should rehabilitate the reputation of the Department of Homeland Security's [DHS] infamous report on right-wing extremism. But if anything, these splits on the right highlight the central problem with the paper. In the words of Michael German, a former FBI agent who now works for the American Civil Liberties Union, the DHS document focuses "on ideas rather than crime"; it was concerned with extremism itself, not with violence, and it gave no sign that you must be violent to meet its definition of "extremist." That approach doesn't just have ominous implications for civil liberties. To the extent that it catches on, it makes it less likely that the members of a group like the SMVM—a militia that felt the need to "keep an eye on" the Hutaree—will be able to cooperate in the fight against bona fide terrorism.

And that leads us to the biggest trouble with the dominant media narrative: It misdirects our attention. The historian Leo Ribuffo coined the term *Brown Scare* to describe a wave of countersubversive activity in the 1930s and '40s, when an understandable fear of Nazis unleashed some much less defensible calls for, in Ribuffo's words, "restrictions on the right of native 'fascist' agitators to speak, publish, and assemble." In the process the authorities conflated some very different people together, leading to surveillance not just of German sympathizers but of reputable conservatives. Other historians have identified two subsequent Brown Scares, one in the early '60s and one in the 1990s.

Like the better-known Red Scares [in which left-wingers were accused of being Communists], but pointing rightwards rather than leftwards, a Brown Scare both exaggerates the threats at hand and obscures the distinctions between genuinely violent plotters, radical but peaceful activists, and members of the mainstream.

You can see such a mindset at work in the SPLC's watch list. You can see it in press accounts that blur still more boundaries, so that there seems to be little difference between a terror cell and a Tea Party. You can see it in documents like the Department of Homeland Security's report. You're even beginning to see it in legislation. Late last month the Oklahoma House voted 98-1 to amend a bill that, among other provisions, increased the penalties for recruiting new gang members. Under the revised legislation, the same penalties would befall recruiters for unauthorized militias.

That is where we stand today. We can reenact the Brown and Red Scares of the past, or we can pull back from a mentality that has never been good for either liberty or security; we can plunge further into madness like the Oklahoma bill, or we can adopt the measured skepticism displayed this week by Judge Roberts. Choose wisely.

Periodical and Internet Sources Bibliography

The following articles have been selected to supplement the diverse views presented in this chapter.

Associated Press	"Militia with Neo-Nazi Ties Patrols Arizona Desert, *New York Times*, July 17, 2010. www.nytimes.com.
Barton Gellman	"The Secret World of Extreme Militias," *Time*, September 30, 2010. www.time.com.
Michelle Goldberg	"Why the White Militias Are Back," *Daily Beast* (blog), August 13, 2009. www.thedailybeast.com.
Jared Keller	"Hutaree Militia May Be Released: A Dangerous Decision?," *Atlantic*, May 4, 2010. www.theatlanticwire .com.
Eli Lake	"Federal Agency Warns of Radicals on Right," *Washington Times*, April 14, 2009. www.washingtontimes .com.
New York Times	"The Government and the Militia Movement," March 30, 2010. http://roomfordebate.blogs .nytimes.com.
Mark Potok	"The Disease Is Hate," Southern Poverty Law Center *Intelligence Report*, no. 91, Fall 1998. www .splcenter.org.
Ben Schmitt, Amber Hunt, and David Ashenfelter	"Hutaree: Real Threat or Good Ol' Boys?," *Detroit Free Press*, April 1, 2010. www.freep.com.

What Groups Are Linked to the Militia Movement?

Chapter Preface

One of the most influential civilian militias in United States history is the racist Ku Klux Klan, or KKK. Chip Berlet and Matthew Lyons note in a 1995 article in the *Progressive* that "the most famous militia movement in the United States, the Ku Klux Klan, arose as a citizens' militia during the turmoil of Reconstruction." Formed by ex-Confederates, the KKK was dedicated to overthrowing the nascent Republican Party and preventing blacks from obtaining equal rights in the post–Civil War South. It was a "terrorist organization" that advanced its goals by "murdering blacks—and some whites who were either active in Republican politics or educating black children," according to an article by Richard Wormser that is part of The Rise and Fall of Jim Crow series on PBS.org.

Some writers have linked the KKK to the more modern militia movement. For instance, in Robert S. Levy's 2005 *Antisemitism: A Historical Encyclopedia of Prejudice and Persecution*, David A. Meier's entry on the militia movement states that the militia movement is xenophobic, anti-Semitic, and racist, and that "the movement's social-intellectual outlook owes much to the nineteenth-century Ku Klux Klan (KKK.)" Morris Dees goes further in his 1996 book *Gathering Storm: America's Militia Threat* and argues that the modern militia movement was created by Ku Klux Klan leader Louis Beam.

Dees admits, however, that most in the militia movement are not, like the KKK, avowedly racist. Meier, too, notes that the militia movement and the KKK are distinct, writing that, "contrary to the more public and confrontational style of the KKK, the U.S. militia movement shied away from public exposure in favor of survivalist and isolationist activities."

Michael Moore, in his 2002 film *Bowling for Columbine*, suggests that the National Rifle Association (NRA), an influential gun rights group that has supported the militia movement, had links to the KKK. The NRA strongly rejected this claim in a March 27, 2003, essay on its website, noting that the "NRA was founded by former Union Army officers who fought a war to bring an end to slavery. It would record that Civil War veteran Maj. Gen. Ambrose Burnside was the Association's first president. It would record that the man who signed the act making the Klan an illegal organization later became NRA's eighth president—Ulysses S. Grant."

The following chapter's viewpoints debate the militia movement's possible links to other groups and ideologies, such as the Tea Party, libertarianism, and the NRA itself.

> "The flirtation between nativists and Tea Partyers that began during the healthcare debate last summer, as coverage for illegal immigrants became a flashpoint, has intensified."

The Tea Party Is Linked to the Militia Movement

Gaiutra Bahadur

Gaiutra Bahadur is a freelance journalist and a frequent contributor to the Nation, *an American weekly journal featuring analysis on politics and culture. In the following viewpoint, she discusses collaborations between nativist militia groups and Tea Party factions. Bahadur outlines the growth of these partnerships by detailing events that led to their formations, as well as their overlapping ideologies. She attacks Republican lawmakers for refusing to rein in the Tea Party's flirtation with militias and violence.*

As you read, consider the following questions:

1. Why did the Minuteman Civil Defense Corps dissolve, according to the viewpoint?
2. What, according to the author, is the Tea Party's position on immigration?

Gaiutra Bahadur, "Nativists Get a Tea-Party Makeover" *Nation*, October 28, 2010. http://thenation.com. Reproduced by permission.

3. How has SB-1070, an Arizona law that requires police to ask for proof of legal residency from people they believe to be undocumented immigrants, brought nativists and Tea Party groups together?

In August of 2009, Al Garza, a leader in the anti-immigrant movement, left his post as vice president of the Minuteman Civil Defense Corps (MCDC), once the largest, richest and most politically connected border vigilante group in the country. In an e-mail to supporters, Garza explained: "I do not see an end in sight for the problems plaguing what was once the greatest citizen movement in America."

It had been an embarrassing summer for the group. A former member, Shawna Forde, was arrested and charged with murdering a Latino man and his 10-year-old daughter in Arizona. Forde allegedly believed that she would find drugs and cash in the victim's home, on a dirt road only a few miles from the US-Mexico border. Prosecutors contend that Forde was enacting a delusional plan to fund her breakaway faction—the Washington State–based Minutemen American Defense—by robbing Latin American drug cartels that she imagined were out to get her. The details about her fringe character that later emerged—her interest in starting an underground militia, her string of arrests for prostitution and petty theft, information from a co-defendant that her nickname was "White," because "she hates all ethnicity with the exception of Caucasians"—further wrecked whatever credibility the Minutemen had.

Reinventing the Minutemen

The publicity surrounding the case enabled Garza to recruit hundreds, including former Minutemen, to an alternative group he soon created, The Patriot's Coalition. "A lot of people felt, well, you're a Minuteman, you're a killer," Garza told me, at a truck stop near his home in Cochise County, Arizona. "The name Minuteman has been tainted by organizations that didn't want us at the border, that say we're killers, that we've done harm." Fortunately for Garza and others, their desire to reinvent coincided with a unique opportunity to do so — the emergence of the Tea Party movement on the national political horizon.

A few months before he broke with the Minutemen, Garza met Joanne Daley, his local Tea Party coordinator, at a tax day protest she had organized. Daley was a nexus of conservatism in Cochise County, spearheading health care reform town halls and a chapter of Glenn Beck's 9/12 Project. When Daley met Garza, she said, "we . . . found out we had a lot in common, mostly outrage." And when the time came for Garza to rebrand himself and his cause, he turned to Daley. She had expertise seeding nonprofits, developed through an old job with the state of Arizona. She registered Garza's new group with the Arizona Corporation Commission, listing him as president and herself as a member of the board of directors.

The Minuteman Civil Defense Corps dissolved this past spring, after years of infighting and accusations of financial mismanagement. But the demise of the group, once so mediagenic that it spawned many imitators, does not signal the death of organized nativism in the United States. On the contrary, the anti-immigrant movement is stronger than ever. And it is gaining political muscle through its growing ties to other ultraconservative groups. Like Garza, many nativists are morphing into Tea Party irregulars. They are also redefining themselves more broadly as patriots, embracing a resurgent states rights movement to challenge the federal government's authority.

Consider, for example, the FIRE Coalition, an obscure organization that the Southern Poverty Law Center says accounted for almost all of the significant growth in 2009 in the number of grassroots outfits that harass immigrants. The FIRE Coalition has vilified undocumented immigrants as violent criminals and created a website that allows anyone to inform on them and their employers. But the group went well beyond its original mission in August, when it co-sponsored a national conference in Pennsylvania that brought together gun rights advocates, "Obamacare" opponents and John Birch Society members under the banner of states "demand[ing] their sovereignty from the tyranny of the Federal government." The speakers included Richard Mack, the author of *The County Sheriff: America's Last Hope* and a former Arizona sheriff who is—as conference promoters put it—"teaching local sheriffs that they have the power to say no to federal agents."

Shared Ideology

It's no accident that the group held its conference at Valley Forge [Pennsylvania], scene of George Washington's winter redoubt in 1777. The patriot movement often invokes Revolutionary War imagery to cast itself as a ragtag bunch of ordinary citizens rebelling against a repressive government. The anti-immigrant movement embraces the same rhetoric. FIRE national director Jeff Lewis boasts that as delegate to a "3rd Continental Congress," he drafted "instructions to federal and state governments regarding their numerous usurpations and violations of the US Constitution." Nativists, like Tea Partyers, fly flags bearing the Revolutionary War motto "Don't Tread on Me" at rallies. And of course, the Minutemen sought to exploit the brand of the American Revolution with a knockoff name years before the Tea Party did.

Despite this shared packaging, the Tea Party's position on immigration isn't as clearly defined as on the deficit or healthcare. One of the movement's few recognizable leaders—former House majority leader Dick Armey, a major Tea Party organizer as chair of the small-government nonprofit FreedomWorks—received a C-minus for his Congressional record from NumbersUSA. He even lamented on national television the presence of infamous immigrant-baiter Tom Tancredo in the Tea Party. A Gallup poll earlier this year [2010] indicated that significantly more Tea Party backers feel seriously threatened by terrorism and the size of the federal government than by illegal immigration.

Nonetheless, the flirtation between nativists and Tea Partyers that began during the healthcare debate last summer, as coverage for illegal immigrants became a flashpoint, has intensified. The lines between the movements are blurring, as members overlap at the grassroots and leaders make official appearances at each other's events. Roy Beck, executive director of NumbersUSA, spoke at the Tea Party's first convention in February. "There's a whole lot of cross-pollination between the Tea Party movement and the anti-immigrant movement," says Marilyn Mayo, co-director of right-wing research for The Center on Extremism at the Anti-Defamation League, which monitors nativist groups. "We're starting to see a lot of focus on immigration in the Tea Party. It's the next step for them after healthcare."

SB-1070, the Arizona law that requires police to ask for proof of legal residency from people they believe could be undocumented immigrants, has been a catalyst. Activism around the law this summer showcased the chemistry between nativists and various Tea Party groups. The Tea Party Patriots gathered thousands of signatures in favor of the law. The Tea Party Nation co-sponsored a rally in Phoenix on June 5, which proclaimed the backing of the broader patriot movement. The slogans on the T-shirts and buttons for sale there broadcast a wide array of messages and causes not related to immigration, including: "Dictators Prefer Armed Citizens" and "Karl Marx Was Not A Founding Father." An overwhelming 88 percent of Tea Party "true believers" in Washington also back the law, according to a University of Washington poll.

Many nativists argue that the Tea Party's emphasis on fiscal conservatism suits their own argument that immigrants here illegally drain the public's pocketbook. But why would anti-immigrant activists want to merge with a movement with a stance on immigration that is still up for debate? And more fundamentally, why would a movement that constantly howls that the federal government isn't doing enough (to enforce the country's borders) court a movement dedicated to limiting the role of the federal government?

To understand what they see in each other, consider the common ground between Daley and Garza. They both contend that President Obama has not yet proved that he is a US citizen. Both are open to conspiracy theories. In addition to being a birther, Garza believes Mexico is using its migrants as part of a Reconquista plot, abetted by some Latino members of Congress, to take back the southwestern United States. "Illegal aliens," he said, "are considered to be their silver bullet or choice of weapon, if you will, to make change in the United States." And Garza and Daley both embrace a resurgent states rights movement. It is the terrain on which those who think the federal government is too active and those who think it isn't active enough meet, despite the apparent ideological contradiction.

Fighting the Feds

That terrain also overlaps neatly with the mesquite borderlands of Arizona, which is—in the words of a now-iconic bumper sticker depicting Gov. Jan Brewer flexing her muscles, as Rosie the Riveter—"Doing the Job the Feds Won't Do." The state is fighting the feds in court, as it contests a lawsuit accusing it of violating the US Constitution by attempting to do what only the federal government can do: regulate the country's borders and, thus, make immigration law. It's no surprise that inhabitants of Nobama-Land, including Tea Party and patriot groups, would find common cause with this brandishing of states rights. Opposition to the federal healthcare law, especially the mandate that every individual get insurance, has been framed as an issue of state sovereignty by those groups. Arizona led the backlash there too, as the first state to call for a ballot initiative to outlaw compelling health coverage. . . .

States rights are being invoked now to a degree that they haven't been since desegregation. At least 11 other states are considering versions of Arizona's immigration law, and thirty-eight

"Tea Party Dictionary, Militias," cartoon by Shelly Matheis. www.CartoonStock.com. Copyright © Shelly Matheis. Reproduction rights obtainable from www.CartoonStock.com.

other states are considering measures to opt out of aspects of the healthcare law. The Tenth Amendment Movement, which pushes state sovereignty on a whole host of divisive issues, is winning adherents in both Tea Party and nativist circles. It appeals both to those who argue the federal government refuses to do what it should and those who argue it shouldn't do what it is.

This affinity with the Tea Party, to the extent that it also leads to backing from a movement with growing political momentum and grassroots energy, promises to lend more clout to anti-immigrant leaders. Take the victory of a dark horse candidate for state assembly in California. The odds were so long for Tim Donnelly—a former Minuteman leader who runs his family's plastics supply business in Twin Peaks—that he couldn't even hire a campaign consultant. But various Tea Party groups went to work for him, and in July he managed to win the Republican primary in a district that votes Republican. He said he couldn't have won without Tea Party volunteers walking precincts and knocking on doors. "It was the way we reached people," he said. "We didn't have the money to reach people in the conventional way." Donnelly said he realized, in the crush of a crowd of thousands at a tax protest in 2009, that the Tea Party movement would far outstrip the Minutemen in reach. It has allowed him to situate anxiety about undocumented workers in the context of a broader anger against a federal government he compared to "King George who kept taxing us, taxing us, taxing us, but never wanted to hear from us." Donnelly campaigned on reproducing Arizona's immigration law in California. It is first on his agenda if elected.

Nativist causes are getting a wider hearing, as Tea Party groups meet with political candidates from every party and at every level. Daley's Tea Party group in Cochise County, for instance, pushed for every statewide, county and local candidate who sought its support—and she says there have been many—to adopt a tougher stance on border security. Connections to the patriot movement have also broadened the base for anti-immigrant politics. "You have people who entered the Tea Party movement largely over fiscal issues getting into a whole realm of politics that they were not really . . . involved in," says the Southern Poverty Law Center's Heidi Beirich, who tracks the ties between the anti-immigrant and patriot movements.

Maladjusted Misfits

The evolution of Jeff Schwilk, an ex-Marine and Minuteman leader from northern San Diego County who has also jumped on the patriot bandwagon, suggests another, more subtle reason all the cross-pollination matters.

The group he founded, the San Diego Minutemen, adopted an aggressive style that landed its members in court several times and led the *San Diego Union-Tribune* to call them "maladjusted misfits." They provoked physical confrontations at work sites that led to misdemeanor arrests in a few cases. In one case, police charged Minuteman John Monti with beating up a day laborer and filing a false report alleging that the laborers attacked him. A defamation suit that Monti settled claims that he, with Schwilk's help, distributed "Wanted" flyers with mug shots of the immigrant workers and a number for the San Diego police. Meanwhile, a jury in a civil case found Schwilk guilty of slandering a Korean-American ACLU observer by circulating a link to a website that suggested she helped day laborers because they paid her for sex.

But there has been a marked change in the style and presence of Schwilk's group in the past year. Members of the San Diego Hate Crimes Coalition say the group's in-your-face antics peaked in 2007 and 2008. Day laborers still occasionally see a few of the men they call "los racistas," who used to dog them, but the Minutemen keep their distance now. Their numbers are also much diminished. "It's not as aggressive as it used to be, when they came out in force, with dogs," said Ernesto Hernandez, a day laborer waiting for work at a shopping center in Vista, California one morning this summer.

The San Diego Minutemen appear to have shifted strategy, to capitalize on a movement with electoral buzz and a reputation less compromised than their own. In 2009, Schwilk started the SoCal Patriots Coalition, a loose network that claims local Tea Party and gun rights groups as members. He has also participated in several open-carry exercises. "Our fight is all political now," Schwilk e-mailed me. "Our fight is in our cities, county and state, and federal governments." A group once listed as a SoCal Patriots member—StopTaxingUs.com, a key organizer of the anti-immigrant rallies in Phoenix this summer—also seems to be trying to shed its past connections to the San Diego Minutemen. Immigrant advocates say Rhonda Deniston, a StopTaxingUs .com coordinator, was once an active member. (She denied ever being involved with Schwilk's group in an e-mail.) She is now a Tea Party organizer in San Diego County. Schwilk and Deniston both denied requests for interviews.

As it reinvents as an arm of the patriot movement, the San Diego Minutemen also appears to be packaging its hate in a more sophisticated way. "We suspect that all these groups they hook up with, they share know-how and tactics," says Capt. Miguel Rosario, whose precinct includes a canyon targeted by Minutemen because migrant tomato pickers lived there. The Minutemen had crusaded against the camp as a den of child prostitution for years. In October of 2009, Schwilk and two men called Immigration and Customs Enforcement to report a case of underage prostitution in the canyon. When police arrived, they found the Minutemen armed with cans of mace and a stun gun. In their custody were a 29-year-old woman and a migrant. The Minutemen claimed the migrant attacked one of them, but it was the migrant who bore the bruises. Police charged two of the Minutemen with battery, but dropped the case because the victim, who is undocumented, disappeared. Schwilk was not charged, because he delegated to the others, Rosario said.

The case indicated to the precinct captain that Schwilk was beginning to subcontract out his rhetoric as well his rough-housing. After charging the Minutemen with misdemeanors, he was deluged with hate-filled e-mails accusing him of being a Reconquista agent. But none came directly from Schwilk or any member of his organization. "We can see progressively how they get more politically astute about how to talk and how to act," Rosario said. "They've evolved from saying anything to now being very careful about what they say."

A Chance to Reinvent Themselves

While the Tea Party movement contains fringe characters to rival the anti-immigrant radical right, the intensifying relationship between the two has given some nativist groups and leaders with troubled pasts the opportunity to recreate themselves in a more mainstream image. It also threatens to boost anti-immigrant mea-sures in play at state and local governments across the country, as the Tea Party's recent successes at the polls lead more moderate Republicans to also consider recreating themselves in their image.

> *"A series of reports . . . attempting to
> connect the Tea Party movement
> with domestic terrorists in the militia
> movement shows how desperate the left
> has become trying to stop the political
> juggernaut."*

The Tea Party Is Not Linked to the Militia Movement

John Rossomando

John Rossomando is a journalist whose work has been featured in numerous media, such as CNSNews.com, Newsmax, and Crisis. *In the following viewpoint, he reports that the Southern Poverty Law Center (SPLC) has attempted to link the Tea Party to radical militia groups, racism, and violence. He argues that there is no evidence for these charges and that the Tea Party is a patriotic and nonviolent group. He interviews Tea Party leaders and supporters who argue that the SPLC is simply a liberal group attempting to discredit those on the right.*

As you read, consider the following questions:

1. What speakers at Tea Party gatherings has the SPLC singled out, and what has it accused them of, according to Rossomando?

2. What did Sarah Palin say at the Tea Party Convention in Nashville that worried the SPLC, according to the author?

3. According to Rossomando, what does New York governor George Pataki think of the Tea Party?

Tea Party leaders say a series of reports by the Southern Poverty Law Center (SPLC) attempting to connect the Tea Party movement with domestic terrorists in the militia movement shows how desperate the left has become trying to stop the political juggernaut.

The group says individuals such as [conservative TV commentator and author] Glenn Beck, former Alaska Gov. Sarah Palin and Minnesota Rep. Michele Bachmann—all regulars at major Tea Party gatherings—have given widespread visibility for ideas espoused by the militia movement, or the "Patriot movement" as SPLC calls it.

According to SPLC, the Patriot movement—largely comprised of white supremacists—was animated in the 1990s by a shared view of the federal government as the enemy and a belief the Federal Emergency Management Agency [FEMA] secretly runs concentration camps.

"The 'tea parties' and similar groups that have sprung up in recent months cannot fairly be considered extremist groups, but they are shot through with rich veins of radical ideas, conspiracy theories and racism," Mark Potok, director of the SPLC's Intelligence Project, wrote in a piece titled "Rage On The Right: The Year In Hate And Extremism" from the group's Spring 2010 edition of its *Intelligence Report.*

SPLC also sees a connection between the "paranoid" antigovernment ideas espoused by extremist militias, racist skinheads, and the ideas espoused by prominent Tea Partiers.

Accordingly, Palin's February [2010] speech before the National Tea Party Convention in Nashville, Tenn., where she said "America is ready for another revolution" features alongside events such as the Oklahoma City bombing [in 1995 that killed 168 people] and the uncovering of various attempted militia terror plots since the 1990s in SPLC's Patriot movement timeline.

Similarly, SPLC accuses Bachmann of giving "even the most paranoid militiaman a run for his money" on account of her stances against cap and trade because she jokingly told a radio show: "I want people in Minnesota armed and dangerous on this issue of the energy tax because we need to fight back."

SPLC attacks Beck for having run a series of segments on his show for entertaining the idea FEMA runs concentration camps prior to debunking them, which it insinuates puts the popular host in the same category as the followers of the militia movement and other extremists.

A Desperate Effort

Bachmann dismisses SPLC's attacks as a "desperate" effort to discredit the Tea Party movement because of its effectiveness.

"Clearly the Tea Party is a threat to the radical left. It has become clear that anybody who opposes the [President Barack] Obama agenda is part of the Tea Party," Bachmann said in an e-mailed statement to *The Daily Caller* [*TheDC*]. "The Tea Party is a movement not a political party, it is Republicans, Democrats, libertarians, constitutional party individuals and everyone in between. It is full of political and apolitical individuals, who all deeply care for our nation and are opposed to the liberal agenda takeover.

Bachmann continued: "The Tea Party goes after the ideology of out-of-touch liberals like President Obama and Speaker [of the House] Nancy Pelosi, yet when it comes to liberals going after Tea Party activists, they focus on personal politics of destruction. Liberals are desperate, they are up against the wall and will stop at nothing to discredit this great grassroots movement that represents Americans who are fed up with this administration."

Former New York Gov. George Pataki, who runs a group called Revere America, likewise believes the SPLC articles equal an effort to frighten voters.

"From the beginning, they've tried discrediting," Pataki told *TheDC*. "They've been pretending that all of those who are so upset with the direction of Washington have somehow been paid to show up rather than being patriotic Americans who are very unhappy with the course of Washington.

"Then they tried to portray it as a violent group when it wasn't, and now they portray it as a racist group and it's not. To me it's sad that they would dismiss what is truly an expression of American democracy."

Other Tea Party leaders also see irony in SPLC's claims [that] the movement and its leaders are "paranoid" and looking for conspiracies because they fail to confront their own conspiracy theories.

"That seems to me to be exactly what the SPLC is doing in this case," said Let Freedom Ring President Colin Hanna, a regular speaker at Tea Party events. "There is no credible evidence of any such alleged extremism in the rather idealistic and morally American Tea Party movement that has emerged in the last year or two."

SPLC declined to comment.

> *"Many early Americans believed that those willing to undertake the duty of freemen to defend liberty and the constitutional order against the state exemplified the ideal of patriotic citizenship."*

The Militia Movement Has Libertarian Roots

Robert H. Churchill

Robert H. Churchill is a professor of history at the University of Hartford in Connecticut. In the following viewpoint, he argues that the militia movement of the 1990s was linked to a libertarian interpretation of the American Revolution. This interpretation held that it was a patriotic duty to resist government tyranny with force, Churchill contends. Churchill notes that this interpretation of the American Revolution disappeared from mainstream discussion but was adopted by far-right groups. Thus, he maintains, the militia movement can be seen as a legitimate heir to some of the libertarian ideas of the American Revolution.

As you read, consider the following questions:

1. Who was Norm Olson and what did he believe, according

Robert H. Churchill, "Introduction," *To Shake Their Guns in the Tyrant's Face*. Ann Arbor: University of Michigan Press, 2009, pp. 5–11. Copyright © University of Michigan Press. All rights reserved. Reproduced by permission.

to Churchill?

2. What does the author think about the argument that the militia movement was inspired by racism or economic troubles?

3. What does Churchill say happened to Independence Day celebrations over the course of the twentieth century?

On April 29, 1994, twenty-eight men met in the woods of northern Michigan. Angered by the events at Ruby Ridge [the site in Idaho of a violent confrontation between federal agents and the Randy Weaver family] and Waco [a confrontation in Texas between federal officials and the Branch Davidians that ended in seventy-six people dying] and alarmed by rumors of black [i.e., covertly operating] helicopters and foreign soldiers hidden on American military bases, these men agreed to associate as the first brigade of the Northern Michigan Regional Militia. The militia was the brainchild of Norm Olson and Ray Southwell, the pastor and deacon of a small Baptist church near Alanson, Michigan. Those assembled elected Olson as their commander. He in turn laid down some basic principles under which they would proceed. First, the militia would operate publicly. If they believed that the government was a threat to their liberty, then it was their duty, as patriots and as men, to "shake their guns in the tyrant's face." Second, the militia would be open to men and women of principle regardless of race or faith. Olson believed that the government was utterly corrupt, but unlike other voices on the far right, he argued that the source of that corruption lay in the human heart and not in any Jewish conspiracy or in the loss of racial purity.

Minutemen Reincarnated

Finally, Olson portrayed the militia as an expression of popular sovereignty, a reincarnation of the Minutemen who had faced off against the [English] king's troops at Lexington and Concord

[Massachusetts]. The people's right to associate under arms to protect their liberty, Olson declared, was not subject to regulation by any government on earth. The purpose of that association was to create an armed force capable of deterring an increasingly abusive government. That April 29 meeting proved to be the genesis of the Michigan Militia. . . .

Some of these emerging militias followed Olson's model of holding public meetings and opening membership to all citizens. Others disagreed. The Militia of Montana, which began organizing in February 1994, offered a very different model. Founder John Trochman warned that America faced an apocalyptic invasion by the forces of the New World Order and consequently proposed an organizational structure based on closed, underground cells. This more nativist and millenarian vision of the movement also spread to the Midwest. The Militia of Montana's manual was adopted by the early leadership of the Ohio Unorganized Militia. Mark Koernke, whose vision was similar to Trochman's, also began organizing local underground militias in southeast Michigan.

By the spring of 1995, hundreds of militias with as many as one hundred thousand members total had formed across the nation. Most of the public became aware of the burgeoning militia movement only in the aftermath of the Oklahoma City bombing on April 19, 1995. Around the country, people reacted with shock, wondering what could possibly motivate citizens who claimed to be patriots to take up arms against their own democratically elected government. As journalists, self-appointed militia experts, and scholars rushed to offer answers, several explanations emerged. A loose coalition of civil rights organizations argued that the movement was an outgrowth of a white supremacist paramilitary movement that had emerged in the 1980s, and constituted an attempt to reestablish white supremacy by armed force. Other experts saw the movement as the product of millenarian impulses within the Christian Right. Finally, some scholars and journalists compared the militia movement to earlier populist vigilante movements, and argued that it was the product of economic dislocation. All of these explanations portrayed the movement as an outgrowth of right-wing extremism in America.

Are They Extremists?

Like most Americans, I first learned of the militia movement in the weeks after the Oklahoma City bombing. As I began to do research on the movement, I became increasingly dissatisfied with these explanations. From the outset, I was struck by the lack of evidence behind the charge that racism had played a significant role in the emergence of the movement. It was also clear to me that economic concerns did not hold a prominent place in the movement's analysis of the ills facing the nation. Finally, while some militias were clearly caught up in the sort of elaborate conspiracy theories that characterized American millenarian movements in the twentieth century, others went out of their way to debunk such theories.

Beyond this empirical unease, it seemed to me as a historian that the concept of extremism begged a question: how do certain ideas, movements, and political impulses come to be considered extremist? As a citizen whose political identity was shaped by the late twentieth century, I saw the militias' assertion of a right to use armed force to change government policy as new, threatening, and beyond the pale of legitimate politics. But as a historian of early America I found achingly familiar their assertion of a right to take up arms to prevent the exercise of unconstitutional power by the federal government. As a historian, then, I was faced with a more specific question: how has the United States as a political society come to view the assertion of that right as extremist?

Why did the militia movement emerge in 1994, and why do we view that movement as extremist? On the surface they are simple questions, and yet answering them involved reading the hundreds of newsletters and Web pages in which militia men and women explained their movement to the public, to each other, and to themselves. It involved hours of interviewing participants around the country, of sitting down and asking them what they were trying to do and listening carefully to the answers. Finally, it required tracing the history of the ideas that animated the movement, with a particular focus on the impact of those ideas on previous insurgent movements and on the relationship of these movements to the established political parties of their day.

As I listened to the disparate voices within the militia movement, the issue of political violence stood out above all others: the proximate cause of the movement lay in its members' perception that their government had turned increasingly violent. That perception may have been exaggerated, but it was firmly rooted in reality and fundamental to militia members' sense of their place in the world. The excesses committed by the federal government at Ruby Ridge, Idaho, and Waco, Texas, were the most important events driving this perception. But many joining the movement perceived a general trend at all levels of law enforcement toward the use of paramilitary tactics and military hardware, and several reported violent assaults and sieges reminiscent of Waco in their local communities. Finally, militia men and women feared that recently passed federal gun control legislation would be enforced with the same violence exhibited at Waco and Ruby Ridge. They feared that as gun owners they might become "next year's Davidians."

The Militia of Association

To defend themselves against what they perceived to be an imminent threat, a broad array of libertarians, gun owners, Christian millenarians, and survivalists seized upon the militia of association, an old political institution with a hallowed place within the collective memory of the founding period propagated by the gun rights movement. To explain the legitimacy of their new militia movement, members turned to ideas about political violence with similar eighteenth-century origins: they argued that popular political violence was a legitimate response to the denial of certain fundamental rights by agents of government; that insurgent violence against the state was a legitimate response to state-sponsored violence against its citizens; and that a state monopoly on violence, absent any popular deterrent against its abuse, yielded more violence rather than less.

In support of these assertions, the militia movement invoked one of the most radical intellectual legacies of the American Revolution. When Americans of the founding generation debated the limits of the right of revolution, two theories of legitimate political violence emerged. The first held that armed resistance to the oppressive acts of a representative government became legitimate only when that government infringed the constitutional means of opposition, such as access to the courts and the ballot box. But a second, more radical understanding of the meaning of the revolutionary conflict with Great Britain justified armed resistance to the acts of any government that repeatedly violated those rights, liberties, and privileges that the people believed they possessed as human beings and as citizens of a constitutional republic. Such transgressions of liberty were deemed illegitimate even if they had been enacted by a representative government following proper constitutional procedures. Under this theory, it was not only the right, but the duty, of all free men to embody themselves in a militia of the whole community and nullify the offending acts, by armed force if necessary. Many early Americans believed that those willing to undertake the duty of freemen to defend liberty and the constitutional order against the state exemplified the ideal of patriotic citizenship.

The eighteenth-century proponents of this ideal of patriotic insurgency based their claims for its legitimacy upon a particular interpretation of the meaning of the American Revolution. They described the Revolution not as a struggle for representation or to create an independent nation, but as a struggle to defend liberty against a corrupt and abusive state. I will refer to this interpretation as the *libertarian* understanding of the American

Revolution. This interpretation was libertarian in the sense that it portrayed the Revolution as a struggle to protect liberty by enforcing inviolable constitutional restraints on the power of the state. Nevertheless, the early American proponents of this theory believed that liberty was best protected by a united community, and that an individual's freedom to act on behalf of either the people or the state was subject to the approval of the local community. They believed that the recourse to legitimate violence was neither public, in the sense of requiring state sanction, nor wholly private. This theory thus had little connection to the hyperindividualism of modern economic libertarianism.

The Libertarian American Revolution

In the 1790s, this libertarian understanding of the meaning of the American Revolution found its way into the ideas, rituals, and institutions of the Democratic-Republican Party. Over the next several decades, Democratic-Republican political culture and political rhetoric celebrated the Revolution as a legitimate exercise of popular violence against a despotic government. After the passing of the Revolutionary generation, the libertarian understanding of the Revolution retained a significant place within the collective memory of the Democratic Party. During the Civil War this libertarian memory of the Revolution fueled both political opposition and violent resistance to the war policies of the [Abraham] Lincoln administration.

In the last decades of the nineteenth century, however, the libertarian understanding of the American Revolution gave way in collective memory and public commemoration to a new ideal of patriotism and a new set of rituals emphasizing unquestioning loyalty and obedience to the nation-state. Within this new ideology of "one hundred percent Americanism," all forms of revolution took on the visage of an alien, subversive menace. So pervasive was this shift in patriotic ideology that in twentieth-century Independence Day festivities, celebrations of the justified recourse to popular violence against a lawful government

Gun Rights and Militias in Early America

On April 19, 1775, the town of Concord, Massachusetts, was the scene of an interesting confrontation. After the militia of Concord and the surrounding towns had driven the British back from the North Bridge, some of the militiamen began to disperse. The wife of Nathan Barrett, captain of one of Concord's militia companies, spotted one of her husband's men skedaddling home. She went out of her house to confront him, and when he explained that he was feeling ill, she responded that he must not take his gun with him. When he replied simply, "Yes, I shall," she exclaimed, "No, stop, I must have it." The militiaman refused and began to walk off. Mrs. Barrett gave chase, but her quarry was too quick.

The confrontation between Mrs. Barrett, speaking for the community of Concord, and the militiaman captures the clash of community obligation, public safety, private interests, and individual rights that lies at the heart of the legal and historical debate over the meaning of the Second Amendment. For Mrs. Barrett, the militiaman's gun represented his duty to join with his neighbors and bear arms in the collective defense of the community. The militiaman did not dispute that obligation: he had turned out with his neighbors to defend the town and headed home only after his company had dispersed. But in his eyes the right to retain possession of the gun transcended its importance in allowing him to meet his communal obligation. The gun was his, and he believed he had a right to keep it.

Robert H. Churchill, Law and History Review, *Spring 2007.*

bent on tyranny were entirely replaced by sanitized commemorations of the birth of the nation.

Deprived of its former place in public discussion and commemoration, the libertarian memory of the Revolution lived on at the extremes of the political spectrum. On the far right, the libertarian vision of righteous popular revolution blended with vigilante impulses rooted in white supremacy and the long history of American nativism. This fusion produced a series of paramilitary insurgencies, including the Depression-era Black Legion, and the Minutemen of the 1960s. On the far left, the libertarian justification of armed defense against state tyranny motivated radical civil rights activists such as Robert F. Williams to form local African American militias in the 1950s and 1960s. Within mainstream politics, however, the patriotic emphasis on countersubversion facilitated campaigns to suppress first communists, then fascists, and, after World War II, white supremacists and radical civil rights activists such as Williams. Their willingness to resort to violence against the state marked all of these groups as extremist and un-American.

If the rise of American anticommunism played a key role in further driving the libertarian memory of the Revolution from the public sphere, the defeat of Communism opened the door to its return. In post–Cold War America, a wave of state-sponsored violence, real and imagined, encouraged some Americans to look at the American Revolution through new eyes. Some encountered the libertarian memory of the Revolution in a set of eighteenth-century texts that were widely disseminated by the gun rights movement. Others came across it as an idea articulated within far right discourse, where it was still entwined with white supremacist and nativist corollaries. From these encounters emerged distinct constitutional and millenarian wings of the militia movement, represented respectively by Norm Olson and John Trochman. Though operating on very different principles, these militias together rested on ideas about constitutionalism and political violence, on rituals of public armed deterrence, and

on the eighteenth-century institution of the militia of association. Thus, in terms of ideology, organization, and cultural per-
formance, the militias began in 1994 to do something that was
both very old and very new.

> "There is at least a considerable body of
> circumstantial evidence to suggest that
> [display of third political party bumper
> stickers] will be interpreted by some if
> not many individual police officers in
> exactly the way that Libertarians fear it
> will be."

Linking Libertarians to Extremist Militias Is Dangerous

Steve Newton

Steve Newton is a professor of history at Delaware State University. In the following viewpoint, he argues that a Missouri Information Analysis Center report on the militia movement targets Libertarians in a dangerous manner. He says that Missouri law enforcement unfairly and perhaps illegally collects information about individuals. He also notes that some Missouri law enforcement materials have suggested that Libertarians and those who vote for third-party candidates are dangerous. He concludes that there is reason for concern that Missouri law enforcement may target Libertarians based on their political beliefs.

As you read, consider the following questions:

1. According to Janet Napolitano, as cited by the author, what is the reason the US has fusion centers?

2. What does Newton say that James Keathley did illegally in regard to sex offender information?

3. According to Newton, how many citizens voted for the Libertarian Party candidate, the Constitution Party candidate, or Ron Paul in 2008?

I get sick and tired of the repetitive nature of viral, repeating internet stories that fail to add anything new to a story besides innuendo and personal spin. This is particularly the case since all the MSM [mainstream media] outlets and most of the blogs are now running with pretty much only the brief *Columbia [MO] Daily Tribune* story on the issue of that controverisal Missouri Information Analysis Center [MIAC] report on the Modern Militia Movement.

The Official Response

Let's start there, however, because what interests me is the official response to the story:

> State law enforcement officials said the report is being misinterpreted. Lt. John Hotz of the Missouri State Highway Patrol said the report was compiled by the Missouri Information Analysis Center based in Jefferson City and comes purely from publically available, trend data on militias. . . .
>
> "All this is an educational thing," Hotz said of the report. "Troopers have been shot by members of groups, so it's our job to let law enforcement officers know what the trends are in the modern militia movement."
>
> The report's most controversial passage states that militia "most commonly associate with third-party political groups" and support presidential candidates such as Ron Paul, former

Constitutional Party candidate Chuck Baldwin and Bob Barr, the Libertarian candidate last year [2008]. . . .

The document, according to all reports, was leaked by two Missouri law enforcement officers. The timing is interesting, because of the proximity of that release to the 2009 National Fusion Center Conference, held in (guess what!) Kansas City, MO, from 10–12 March 2009.

Funny that you haven't seen any public mention of this report in conjunction with that convention's ongoing activities, especially this workshop on 11 March:

Identifying Behavioral Indicators as a Precursor to Terrorist Activities

(Baseline Capabilities: I.A.4, I.A.5, and I.B.1)

Session Overview:

This session provides a comprehensive examination of warnings and indicators preceding terrorist activities and how to identify early warning signs often exhibited by criminal extremists. Information sharing is a key component of this session. This session will stress that attacks are planned and that this planning stage is law enforcement's best opportunity to prevent an attack. This session will also provide information on international terrorists and extremists.

Takeaways:

Recognize, identify, and understand various indicators and warning signs exhibited by terrorists and extremists.

Understand the need for and importance of collecting and disseminating actionable intelligence.

Gain knowledge of resources currently available that can assist fusion centers.

Understand the importance of safeguarding privacy and civil liberties.

Understand what indicators fit into an analytic program and what to consider when developing and using indicators. . . .

There is nothing inherently wrong with these training sessions. Yet you have to wonder if it was here that the homegrown Missouri Strategic Report on the Modern Militia Movement was not circulating (with its excellent graphics) as an example of what one State's fusion center was capable of producing.

Fusion Centers and Intelligence Sharing

Also missed in all the internet hoopla over the report's leak to the public was the high-profile visit of new Homeland Security Czar Janet Napolitano to the conference, as also reported by the *Columbia News Tribune*:

Homeland Security Secretary Janet Napolitano says fusion centers like one in Jefferson City are the centerpieces of intelligence-sharing efforts to thwart terrorism and other dangerous risks to communities.

After visiting the local center on Wednesday, Napolitano spoke at the National Fusion Center Conference in Kansas City, where she reminded the nearly 1,000 local, state and federal law enforcers and emergency responders that they are the front line in the fight against terror.

"The reason we have Homeland Security, and the reason we have fusion centers, is we did not have the capacity to connect the dots on various bits of information prior to 9/11," she said.

The centers began popping up in 2006 as a way to coordinate information sharing between various agencies regarding terrorist threats, criminal activity and other dangers. Officials say that as of February [2009], 70 centers were either operating or in the process of opening across the country. . . .

While the purpose of the centers is to share and analyze information, they are not in the business of eavesdropping or otherwise violating people's civil rights, Napolitano said. That issue was one of the main conference topics.

"Fusion centers are not domestic spy agencies and not designed to invade the privacy of citizens," she said. . . .

Hold that one thought—"Fusion centers are not domestic spy agencies and not designed to invade the privacy of citizens"—and set the wayback machine for 2007, and the official (public) version of the Missouri annual report on Homeland Security, wherein the MIAC functions are discussed.

First, here's what is said about the MIAC's official function:

The primary function of MIAC is to collect, store, analyze, and disseminate criminal and terrorist intelligence to law enforcement agencies throughout Missouri and the nation. These services are provided free, and law enforcement agencies and their officers are encouraged to utilize the expertise of the MIAC's criminal analysts by contacting the MIAC to receive assistance in their investigations. The MIAC has access to numerous private and public databases that provide investigators a unique enhancement to their investigations.

Now here's how those LEOs [law enforcement officers] used the MIAC in 2006:

The following inquiries were made to the indicated databases in 2007 (figures are for 9½ months):

System/Number of checks
    Accurint 6,872
    Intel Books 125
    Photos 9,300
    Tel Sub 1,299
    Intel 1,049
    Criminal History 8,560

Dept. of Revenue 11,114

FinCen 182

Interpol 13

Employment Security 2,256

Miscellaneous 4,259

NVPS 36

MoSPIN 2,718

Regis 74

ICE 553

R-Dex 158

LENS 365

Notice that this fusion center's largest single client appears to be the Missouri Department of Revenue. . . .

So fusion centers are not used to *snoop* on private citizens, but one of the largest functions of the Missouri Information Analysis Center seems to be providing data for the State to use in collecting deliquent taxes. That's cut down terrorism, for sure. . . .

Missouri's Poor Record

All this talk of keeping everybody safer and stopping terrorism while protecting privacy and civil rights sounds really, really good, until you realize that Missouri law enforcement's record of keeping information where it is supposed to be is . . . not quite perfect.

In June 2008 the Missouri Court of Appeals, Western District, turned down the appeal of Missouri State Highway Patrol [MSHP] Superintendent James Keathley, who had previously lost a case in the Circuit Court of Jackson County MO regarding the MSHP's habit of illegally releasing confidential information on sex offenders. What the court held was that Keathley had illegally [I can say "illegally" here, because that's what the court ruled] required the plaintiffs to register their information for dissemination in the State's sex offender registry, *even though the plaintiffs' convictions occurred at a point prior to the current law being passed and they were not required to register.*

Libertarian and Constitution Party Presidential Vote Totals, 2008

	Nationwide Votes	Electoral Percentage
Bob Barr, Libertarian Candidate	523,686	.40%
Chuck Baldwin, Constitution Candidate	199,314	.15%

TAKEN FROM: Federal Election Commission, "2008 Official Presidential Election Results," January 22, 2009. www.fec.gov/pubrec /fe2008/2008presgeresults.pdf.

In other words, and laying aside any visceral feelings about sex offenders for a moment, the court ruled that the MSHP had illegally taken data to which it was not entitled by law and then placed it in law enforcement databases.

Here's a snippet of the appellate ruling:

> In his third point on appeal, Mr. Keathley continues to claim that the trial court erred in ordering the defendants to expunge Mr. Doe from all sex offender registries and to delete any personal information pertaining to Mr. Doe obtained as a result of his past registration as a sex offender. He argues that retention of the information Mr. Doe provided to the sex offender registries in files accessible only to law enforcement agencies is procedural and does not require Mr. Doe to take any new action or fulfill a new obligation. . . .
>
> He argues it is of no harm to Mr. Doe because it will be available for only law enforcement purposes. He states it will assist in the investigation of future crimes. Mr. Keathley also asserts that the constitutional prohibition on retrospective laws does not apply to statutes dealing only with procedure or remedies.

Mr. Keathley's argument is unpersuasive. Under *Doe v. Blunt*, requiring Mr. Doe to register as a sex offender and provide the information at issue in this appeal was unlawful. In *Doe v. Phillips*, this court found that equity requires not having access to information that was obtained through an unconstitutional statutory provision. The focus is on how the information was obtained; it is not on how the unlawfully obtained information will be used or accessed in the future.

In other words, Keathley and the MSHP have, in at least one proven case, illegally added information about American citizens to law enforcement databases, such as those used by the MIAC and shared with fusion centers across the country.

But since those databases are secret, how would anybody else be able to challenge the legality of the material in them?

[This is hardly the first action of its sort for abuse of power brought against the MSHP; a brief scan located another detailed complaint about illegal and intrusive roadblocks leading into national forest areas authorized by Keathley's predecessor, Fred Mills, who was nationally considered something of an expert on—you guessed it—combating the militia movement.]

Superintendent Keathley makes no bones about the reliance of Missouri LEOs on the data generated by MIAC:

All public safety information and intelligence is monitored and disseminated to the proper agencies and personnel from the MIAC 24 hours a day.

Missouri Militias

In one sense, I cannot fault Missouri law enforcement for some of its anxiety. Missouri has seen militia violence, anti-abortion violence, and has the misfortune to have the utter nutcases of the Westboro Baptist Church [of Rev. Fred Phelps] in nearby Kansas ("God Hates Fags!"). . . .

So now we come back full circle to the MIAC report on the Militia Movement leaked last week [March 2009]. Many commenters have scoffed at the idea that the information used therein might be for purposes of profiling or to equate third-party supporters with domestic terrorists.

And certainly the language of the report is potentially ambiguous to many:

Common militia symbols

Political and anti-government rhetoric:

Political paraphernalia: Militia members most commonly associate with 3rd party political groups. It is not uncommon for militia members to display Constitutional Party, Campaign for Liberty, or Libertarian material. These members are usually supporters of former Presidential Candidates: Ron Paul, Chuck Baldwin, and Bob Barr.

Anti-government propaganda: Militia members commonly display picture, cartoons, bumper stickers that contain anti-government rhetoric. Most of this material will depict the FRS [federal reserve system], IRS [Internal Revenue Service], FBI, ATF [Bureau of Alcohol, Tobacco, Firearms, and Explosives], CIA, UN, Law Enforcement and "The New World Order" in a derogatory manner. Additionally, racial, anti-immigration, and anti-abortion material may be displayed by militia members.

Militia symbols:

[There are nine flags/crests in this section with short write-ups; only the one quoted next has any specific reference to Missouri]

1st BN/3rd BDE MO Militia Patch: Unit patch displayed by Missouri Militia members.

Literature and Media common to the Militia:

[This section lists two films and one book that have been associated with militia membership.]

This is, some have argued, not suggesting that [2008 Libertarian-associated presidential candidate] Ron Paul supporters are militia members, but that militia members are often Ron Paul supporters, which is—by the barest hair—a different proposition.

Or is it?

Demonizing Libertarians

For a glimpse into the way similar material has been greeted in law enforcement circles, here's some excerpts from ADL's [Anti-Defamation League] advice for officers on Surviving a Traffic-Stop with an Anti-Government Extremist (apparently published in the late 1990s, but still maintained on their website). . . .

> How can an officer tell if he or she is about to have to deal with an anti-government extremist? Sometimes there are no signs at all. But often there are clues that an observant officer can use to help him or her gauge the seriousness of the situation. Ignoring or failing to comprehend these clues can be very dangerous. . . .
>
> Some of the warning signs are obvious; others, less so. Here are some indications that an officer may be dealing with an anti-government extremist: . . .
>
> Peculiar bumper stickers. There are bumper stickers and then there are bumper stickers. Some companies market stickers to anti-government extremists and these are readily identifiable. Examples from one company based in St. Marys, Kansas, include: "And the Lord said (Luke 11:46,52) 'WOE to YOU LAWYERS'"; "Free the Slaves, Abolish IRS and the Federal Reserve"; "Our Danger Isn't Fallout—It's Sellout"; "Know Your Enemies: They Are Your Leaders!"; "Real Americans Don't Wear U.N. Blue"; "Joe McCarthy Was Right"; and so on.

Other strange car decorations, including homemade placards and signs in windows or along tailgates. Cars might display "militia identification numbers" on them. . . .

Identifying individuals with this anti-government philosophy is, however, only the first step. Once an officer determines that he or she is involved in some sort of minor or major confrontation with an anti-government extremist, he or she must correctly assess the situation and make decisions that will help to resolve it successfully. Because the nature and type of such confrontations can vary tremendously, the following suggestions are tentatively offered. Some of them are adapted from suggestions made by Assistant Police Chief Roger Bragdon of the Spokane, Washington, Police Department. Chief Bragdon has had years of experience dealing with anti-government extremists.

Caution should reign. Extremists are often volatile and are often very well-armed. Sometimes they may even have friends in separate cars following behind them. An officer should not hesitate to call for backup if he or she thinks that they may be in a situation involving an extremist. And just as important, the officer should wait for that backup to arrive before putting him or herself at risk.

Officers should be alert for the presence of concealed weapons at all times. Weapons may be concealed on the subject's person or in a convenient hiding place. A vehicle may have multiple weapons and hundreds or thousands of rounds of ammunition. If a vehicle has passengers, the officer should be aware that they too may be well armed.

Now go back and examine that suggestion, in Missouri where over 90,000 citizens voted Libertarian, Constitution, or [for] Ron Paul last year [2008], that telling police officers that the presence of a third-party bumper sticker is a significant indicator of militia membership does not increase the risk for everybody concerned. . . .

A Dangerous Dynamic

Here's the unfortunate dynamic set up in this case:

On the one side: the law enforcement mandate to prevent domestic terrorism and the legitimate survival instincts of every police officer in Missouri, added to which there is a real history of anti-abortion and anti-government violence in the *Show Me* State.

On the other side: increasing reliance by law enforcement on secret databases, about which we have significant evidence that (a) they are often used for purposes of tax collection rather than law enforcement; and (b) that Missouri law enforcement has a documented history of placing illegal private information into such databases—information that once is entered cannot be deleted or challenged because the databases themselves are secret. Add to that the fact that law enforcement officers in Missouri and other areas have already been primed to examine items like bumper stickers or anti-government signs as direct evidence that their lives are in danger whenever they approach such a vehicle ("You are the enemy" the MIAC report reminds them).

This is an unhealthy situation, a dangerous situation to say the least, before we even get into privacy and civil liberties issues.

Regardless of the intent of the authors of this report, there is at least a considerable body of circumstantial evidence to suggest that it will be interpreted by some if not many individual police officers in exactly the way that Libertarians fear it will be interpreted.

This is a serious issue, reaching into other states and involving whole homeland security apparatus that we have allowed to be set overtop of this nation since September 2001.

> "The militias' view that the Second
> Amendment protects our other rights,
> by ensuring the potential for armed
> insurrection against the government,
> is indistinguishable from the long-held
> constitutional ideology of the National
> Rifle Association."

The NRA's Link to the Militia Movement Is Dangerous

Dennis A. Henigan

Dennis A. Henigan is vice president of the Brady Center and the author of Lethal Logic: Exploding the Myths That Paralyze American Gun Policy. *In the following viewpoint, he argues that the National Rifle Association (NRA) has encouraged extremist right-wing militia violence. Henigan says that the NRA suggests that the Second Amendment right to bear arms is the ultimate break on government power, allowing citizens to defend themselves from the government through violence. Henigan says that this argument encourages right-wing militias to believe that attacks on government and government agents are constitutionally protected.*

As you read, consider the following questions:

1. According to Henigan, why do those on the violent right believe that the Second Amendment is the Constitution's cornerstone?

2. What did Wayne LaPierre warn in a letter to NRA members shortly before the Oklahoma City bombing, according to the author?

3. Who is Sharron Angle, and what comment of hers does Henigan believe demonstrates the insurrectionist view of the Second Amendment?

This week's [October 11, 2010,] *Time* magazine cover story on "The Secret World of Extreme Militias" sounds an alarm that cannot be ignored. The threat of terrorism is real, but it does not originate with [Islamist terrorist organization] Al Qaeda alone. The danger of homegrown right wing political violence is just as real.

Violence and the Second Amendment

The *Time* article describes, in chilling terms, the proliferation of heavily armed, right wing militias engaged in paramilitary training to resist the perceived "tyranny" of government authority. *Time* notes that although the groups and individuals of the violent right reflect a "complex web" of ideologies, "among the most common convictions is that the Second Amendment—the right to keep and bear arms—is the Constitution's cornerstone, because only a well-armed populace can enforce its rights." For the militias and their ideological soulmates, "any form of gun regulation, therefore, is a sure sign of intent to crush other freedoms."

The connection between the gun control issue and the threat of violence from the right is an important, but largely untold, story. The militias' view that the Second Amendment protects our other rights, by ensuring the potential for armed insurrection against the government, is indistinguishable from the long-held constitutional ideology of the National Rifle Association [NRA].

For decades, NRA leaders have insisted that the Second Amendment is not only about duck hunting or self-defense against criminal attack. Rather, as one NRA official so colorfully put it, "the Second Amendment . . . is literally a loaded gun in the hands of the people held to the heads of government." NRA Executive Director Wayne LaPierre received loud cheers when he told last year's [2009] Conservative Political Action Conference that our rights as Americans mean little unless we are ready to defend them against the government by force of arms: "Freedom is nothing but dust in the wind till it's guarded by the blue steel and dry powder of a free and armed people. . . . Our founding fathers understood that *the guys with the guns make the rules.*"

The *Time* reporter asked one Ohio militia officer what government action the militia is defending against. He replied, "Most likely it will start when the government tries to take our guns." Of course, the NRA stands alone in its ability to inspire hysterical fears of gun confiscation. During the last Presidential campaign [in 2008, in which the Democratic candidate was Barack Obama], the NRA maintained a www.gunbanobama.com website and its delusional rhetoric about the Administration's supposed gun-banning intentions has been unrelenting. Looking forward to the [2010] elections, LaPierre seeks to rally the NRA troops by warning of "dark clouds on the horizon," with Democrats "lying in the weeds in wait to pick their time to destroy this freedom."

Paranoia and Hatred

The determination of NRA leaders to generate paranoia and hatred toward the government has gotten them into trouble before. In a now-infamous fundraising letter sent on April 13, 1995, LaPierre warned his members about the "jack-booted government thugs" of the federal Bureau of Alcohol, Tobacco, Firearms and Explosives [ATF], who have the "power to take away our Constitutional rights, break in our doors, seize our guns, destroy

The Power of the NRA

At every level of government, a powerful lobby, the National Rifle Association (NRA), disproportionately influences gun policy. If it is true, as some have argued, that gun control proponents are overly focused on the NRA as their opponent, their obsession is understandable. In 2001 *Fortune* magazine named the NRA the most powerful lobby in Washington, eclipsing such notable competitors as the American Association of Retired Persons. A 2005 poll of "congressional insiders" by the *National Journal* found that Democrats rated the NRA the "most effective" interest group on Capitol Hill; Republicans ranked it number two. One "insider" hastened to add, "Effective does not necessarily mean ethical." In fact, a 2006 Harris Poll found the NRA one of the most recognizable, and least trusted, public policy organizations in the nation. The NRA's reputation as "least trusted" was reinforced when it was revealed in 2008 that the gun lobby had sponsored a paid spy who had infiltrated various gun control organizations, posed as a committed gun control activist, befriended grieving gun violence victims under false pretenses, and no doubt passed along inside information to the NRA for more than a decade.

Dennis Henigan, Lethal Logic: Exploding the Myths That Paralyze American Gun Policy, *2009.*

our property, and even injure or kill us. . . ." Six days later, as NRA members found this noxious letter in their mail, Timothy McVeigh, convinced that the time to resist federal tyranny had arrived, bombed the federal building in Oklahoma City that housed the local offices of the ATF.

The *Time* article quotes a "self-described colonel" in a Kentucky militia, who channels LaPierre's incendiary rhetoric by predicting war with "the jackbooted thugs of Washington." LaPierre has made a career of spreading the nonsense that the "jackbooted thugs" are always "lying in the weeds" waiting for the chance to take away everyone's guns. It also is revealing that Richard Mack, one of the sheriffs recruited years ago by the NRA to challenge the Brady Bill [a 1993 federal gun control law] in court, is now a hero of the violent right. In an interview with the *Time* reporter, Mack referred to federal agents as "America's gestapo."

What is truly disturbing is that the political influence of the NRA has given its insurrectionist view of the Second Amendment a home in some very high places, particularly within the Republican Party. It's not just Tea Party Republicans [a loosely organized anti-big-government movement] like Nevada Senatorial candidate Sharron Angle, with her call for "Second Amendment remedies," to be used "when our government becomes tyrannical." As the Republican Party has become more and more ideologically "pure" in its support of NRA policy positions, insurrectionist talk has made some surprising appearances.

For me, the most striking example surfaced in the legal briefs filed before the U.S. Supreme Court in the landmark [*District of Columbia v.*] *Heller* Second Amendment case [of 2008]. [George W.] Bush Administration Solicitor General Paul Clement filed a brief which, paradoxically, both infuriated the "gun rights" crowd and endorsed the insurrectionist theory of the Second Amendment. The pro-gun folks were enraged that the Clement brief actually argued for reversal of the D.C. Circuit's ruling striking down the District of Columbia handgun ban. Clement's brief suggested that the case be sent back to the lower court for further fact-finding. Largely unnoticed was Clement's comment that the Second Amendment guarantees "an armed citizenry as a deterrent to abusive behavior by the federal government itself."

The Right to Fire on Federal Agents

This is a remarkable statement by a lawyer for the United States government. Does it not maintain that the potential for citizens to fire upon federal agents is an important constitutional value? Does it not imply that the greatest Second Amendment protection should be given to citizens who are arming themselves against the threat of government abuse, like the right wing militias now training with assault rifles? Does this theory mean that Timothy McVeigh was engaged in constitutionally protected conduct as he built his bomb, because the threat of violence is "a deterrent to abusive government behavior"? It is noteworthy that Mr. Clement, as a private attorney, represented the NRA in the [2010] *McDonald* [*v. Chicago*] case, in which the Supreme Court struck down the Chicago handgun ban.

It will, of course, be loudly protested that the Bush Justice Department did not advocate violence against the government, nor does the NRA and Sharron Angle. This misses the point. The issue is not whether they have advocated violence against the government, but rather whether they have constructed a constitutional justification for violence. When right wing militias, or lone extremists, take that justification seriously, and act on it, no one should be surprised.

> "*Militias of just about* all *stripes tend to rally around the Second Amendment.*"

The Only "Link" Between the NRA and Militias Is Respect for the Second Amendment

Kurt Hofmann

Kurt Hofmann is a former paratrooper and a columnist for the St. Louis Gun Rights Examiner. *In the following viewpoint, he argues against the idea that the National Rifle Association (NRA) and the militia movement are linked to right-wing extremism. He says that the militia movement includes many different ideologies and that many people in it are opposed to violence. He also notes that there was no real connection between the NRA and the 1995 Oklahoma City bombing. He concludes that the right to resist tyranny is constitutional and not extremist.*

As you read, consider the following questions:

1. Why does Hofmann say that militias of all stripes rally around the Second Amendment?
2. According to the author, why could Timothy McVeigh not have been inspired by Wayne LaPierre's fundraising letter?

3. What is Hofmann's answer to the argument that resistance to tyranny is illegitimate?

The [gun control organization the] Brady Campaign's Dennis Henigan, in one of his more or less weekly screeds [personal opinion] in the *Huffington Post*, claimed that the U.S. is threatened by "right wing extremist militias," who along with the NRA [National Rifle Association], subscribe to a "dangerous" view of the role of the Second Amendment. . . .

Henigan borrows heavily from a recent *Time* magazine article, itself full of such lurid proclamations as:

> Readier for bloodshed than at any time since at least the confrontations in the 1990s in Ruby Ridge, Idaho, and Waco, Texas, the radical right has raised the threat level against the President and other government targets. . . .

A Web of Ideologies

What Henigan chose to *really* get off his feed about, though, is the following:

> *Time* notes that although the groups and individuals of the violent right reflect a "complex web" of ideologies, "among the most common convictions is that the Second Amendment—the right to keep and bear arms—is the Constitution's cornerstone, because only a well-armed populace can enforce its rights."

The reference to a "complex web of ideolgies" is, as far as I can tell, a way of admitting, without *really* admitting, that the militia movement consists of many groups who have nothing but loathing for racist "hate groups"—the kind of groups generally presented as being representative of militia attitudes. It probably *is* true that militias of just about *all* stripes tend to rally around the Second Amendment—hardly surprising, given that the 2nd is the one amendment in the Bill of Rights that names the militia as "necessary to the security of a free state" (and didn't Henigan [in an earlier piece] accuse gun rights advocates of editing the militia clause *out* of the Second Amendment, while, ironically, *he* edited the "of the people" part out of it?).

Henigan tied this into his theme of the NRA as the real driving force behind the threat, by bringing up a fund-raising letter from the NRA's Wayne LaPierre, along with the spectre of Timothy McVeigh (15½ years after the Oklahoma City bombing).

> In a now-infamous fundraising letter sent on April 13, 1995, LaPierre warned his members about the "jack-booted government thugs" of the federal Bureau of Alcohol, Tobacco, Firearms and Explosives [ATF]. . . . Six days later, as NRA members found this noxious letter in their mail, Timothy McVeigh, convinced that the time to resist federal tyranny had arrived, bombed the federal building in Oklahoma City that housed the local offices of the ATF.

"No" to Tyranny

The implication, of course, is that McVeigh's atrocity was *inspired* by the letter—sent six days before he committed it—despite the fact that he had been preparing the attack for *months*, and had quit the NRA in disgust (because it *wasn't* "extreme" enough for his tastes).

What's most telling, though, I think, is that anyone who *denies* that it is legitimate to resist, by force of arms, a tyrannical government, *can only* be arguing that resistance to tyranny is *not* legitimate. In other words, we are, apparently, expected to sit here and take it.

I have an answer to that, and in contrast to my usual long windedness, this answer is even more succinct than "Molon Labe."[1] Not two *words*, but two letters: "No."

Note

1. *Molon Labe* means "come and take them," in Greek. It was supposedly the response of the king of Sparta at the Battle of Thermopylae to the Persian army's demand that the Spartans surrender their weapons.

Periodical and Internet Sources Bibliography

The following articles have been selected to supplement the diverse views presented in this chapter.

Andy Barr	"Okla. GOP Rebukes Tea Party 'Militia,'" *Politico*, April 13, 2010. www.politico.com.
D. Burghart and L. Zeskind	"Tea Parties—Racism, Anti-Semitism and the Militia Impulse," Tea Party Nationalism, September 9, 2010. www.teapartynationalism.com.
Brian Doherty	"The American Anti-revolution," *Reason*, April 23, 2010. http://reason.com.
Eric Dondoro	"State Troopers Now Profiling and Targetting Libertarians as Suspected Violent Militia," Zimbio, March 15, 2009. www.zimbio.com.
Stephen Herrington	"Oklahoma to Sponsor Tea Party Militia?," *Huffington Post*, April 14, 2010. www.huffingtonpost.com.
Josh Horwitz	"In Wake of Tucson, NRA Advocates Armed Militia Movement," *Huffington Post*, February 15, 2011. www.huffingtonpost.com.
Militant Libertarian	"Extreme Militias and Our Most Sacred Right," October 9, 2010. http://militantlibertarian.org.
Scott Nance	"Study: NRA Is Stoking Anti-government Fervor Among the Tea Party, Militia Crowd," *Democratic Daily*, April 15, 2010. http://thedemocraticdaily.com.
Peter Suciu	"The Brady Campaign Is Off Base When Saying NRA and Militias Are Soulmates," FirearmsTruth.com, October 12, 2010. www.firearmstruth.com.

**OPPOSING
VIEWPOINTS®
SERIES**

CHAPTER 3

How Is the Militia Movement Related to Constitutional Militias?

Chapter Preface

The 2010 Supreme Court ruling in *McDonald v. Chicago* held that the Second Amendment right to keep and bear arms applied to the states. Thus, state gun regulations must not violate Second Amendment rights. The Court thus determined that gun rights were not just granted to individuals as part of state militias but were individual rights guaranteed by the US Constitution.

Gun rights advocates generally applauded the decision in *McDonald*. Wayne LaPierre and Chris W. Cox, writing on behalf of the National Rifle Association (NRA), said that *McDonald* was a "vindication for the great majority of American citizens who have always believed the Second Amendment was an individual right and freedom worth defending."

Similarly, Robert Verbruggen, writing in a July 7, 2010, article for *National Review*, further argued that the Court's decision emphasizes the importance of gun rights to the due process guaranteed by the Fourteenth Amendment. One way in which southern states attempted to control blacks was by making it illegal for African Americans to own guns. The Fourteenth Amendment, Verbruggen says, was a response to such discriminatory laws. Verbruggen concludes that "whenever we discuss gun control, we need to remember that a government capable of gun control is capable of tyranny. Both the majority opinion and [Justice Clarence] Thomas's concurrence in *McDonald* . . . perform the crucial service of explaining how important that fact was in the wake of the Civil War."

Gun control advocates also found things to like in the decision. In a June 28, 2010, essay on its website, the Brady Center, which advocates for gun control legislation, was pleased that the Court reaffirmed its position "that the Second Amendment does not prevent elected representatives from enacting common-sense gun laws to protect communities from gun violence." The Brady Center noted that, while Chicago's gun ban would have to be rewritten, "the ruling should have little impact" on the rest of the country.

Mahablog also argued in a June 28, 2010, posting that the *McDonald* decision was a reaffirmation of liberal principles, even though the decision could be seen as a victory for conservative gun rights advocates. "This is the same legal principle on which most of the great civil rights decisions of the 20th century were based," the blogger argued, citing school desegregation as one area where individual rights granted by the federal government were used to overrule state regulations. *Mahablog* also notes that gun control is not unpopular, and expresses the hope that "if the NRA gets too aggressive about dismantling gun control laws . . . the day may come when people start to think long and hard about amending the Second Amendment."

The viewpoints in the following chapter look further at gun rights, the Second Amendment, and the implications for militias.

> "History, philology, and logic . . . furnish
> no solid basis for thinking the Second
> Amendment has anything to do with
> the private ownership of guns."

The Second Amendment Applies to Militias, Not Individuals

Robert J. Spitzer

Robert J. Spitzer is a professor of political science at State University of New York at Cortland and the author of Saving the Constitution from Lawyers: How Legal Training and Law Reviews Distort Constitutional Meaning. *In the following viewpoint Spitzer argues that there has been a broad consensus among scholars that the Second Amendment applies to militia rights to bear arms, not to individuals' rights. He says that poor review practices at student law journals have allowed the idea of the individual right to bear arms to gain a foothold. He concludes that the individual gun rights decision in the Supreme Court's* District of Columbia v. Heller *case was based on poor scholarship and poor history.*

As you read, consider the following questions:

1. How many decisions, and of what kind, did the *Heller*

decision sweep aside, according to Spitzer?

2. What does the author say was the first article in a serious publication to argue that the Second Amendment protected an individual right to bear arms?

3. According to Spitzer, decisions by student law journal editors are too often based on what factors?

The momentous [2008] Supreme Court decision *D.C. v. Heller* has for the first time interpreted the Second Amendment's right to bear arms as protecting an individual right for citizens to have guns for personal uses, "such as self-defense within the home," pushing aside the "well regulated militia" basis for this right stipulated in the first half of the amendment's sentence. In sweeping aside four past high court decisions and over forty lower court cases, the five-member majority concluded that the amendment doesn't really mean what it says. But lost in *Heller's* tumult is the origin of this newfound individual right.

Good Lawyers Make Bad Historians

Of all the admittedly incomplete direct evidence pertaining to the meaning of the Second Amendment, including the Bill of Rights debates during the First Congress and many federal court decisions, none of it supports an individualist reading of the right to bear arms. In a cartoonish depiction of the pivotal 1939 [*United States v.*] *Miller* Supreme Court case, Justice Antonin Scalia's majority opinion dispatches it by saying that it only protects ownership of militia weapons, and nothing more. "Beyond that," Scalia writes, *Miller* "provided no explanation" of the Second Amendment, an assertion contradicted by Justice John Paul Stevens' extended quotations from the case in his dissent.

As if to validate the suspicions of many historians that good lawyers make bad historians, Scalia's opinion relies heavily on history-by-assertion, saying for example that "we find no evidence" that the phrase in the Second Amendment "keep and bear arms" "bore a military meaning." No evidence? None? Pulitzer Prize–winning historian Garry Wills, among others, found the phrase "refers to military service"; "arms," Wills said, "means military service in general." "History, philology, and logic," Wills found, "furnish no solid basis for thinking the Second Amendment has anything to do with the private ownership of guns."

While this leaves open the door to reinterpreting the Second Amendment on other bases, it all but slams shut the idea that it has the originalist pedigree that is the fountainhead of the *Heller* decision. Where, then, did this interpretation come from?

Law Journals and the Law

The answer is a law journal article published in 1960 in the *William and Mary Law Review*, written by a student member of the review's editorial board (and life NRA [National Rifle Association] member) where, for the first time, an article in a serious publication offered two new arguments: that the Second Amendment protected an individual right to bear arms for personal self-defense (ignoring, as did Scalia's decision, the common-law tradition enshrining self-defense rights), and that the amendment created a citizen "right of revolution," a right which, according to the author (but not, thankfully, in *Heller*), was lawfully exercised by the South during the Civil War. Most importantly, this article ignored the primary evidence explaining the amendment's meaning—the debates of the First Congress—and also past academic writing.

For a new theory in any field to have integrity, especially in a subject as well-trodden as the Constitution, it must be subjected to the intense scrutiny, before publication, found in any discipline. But this article, like nearly all others in the field of law, was never submitted to peer review by subject matter experts, the gold standard for evaluating the worthiness of new research and ideas in every other field of study. The reason is alarmingly simple: these critical decisions are made by the law students

The Origin of the Second Amendment

The Second Amendment was adopted to protect the right of the people of each of the several States to maintain a well-regulated militia. It was a response to concerns raised during the ratification of the Constitution that the power of Congress to disarm the state militias and create a national standing army posed an intolerable threat to the sovereignty of the several States. Neither the text of the Amendment nor the arguments advanced by its proponents evidenced the slightest interest in limiting any legislature's authority to regulate private civilian uses of firearms. Specifically, there is no indication that the Framers of the Amendment intended to enshrine the common-law right of self-defense in the Constitution.

John Paul Stevens, dissenting opinion in
District of Columbia v. Heller, *June 26, 2008.*

who control law reviews, and who, for all their hard work and diligence, possess no expertise about that which they publish. No other discipline would dream of yielding such control to its students.

This article was not the first academic analysis of the Second Amendment. It had been subject to serious scrutiny in over a dozen articles published in law reviews from the late nineteenth century through the 1950s; all of them endorsed the amendment's militia basis. The 1960 article committed the egregious error of not citing any of this past writing (much less confronting its arguments), yet it was the seed from which sprouted dozens of subsequent law journal articles which eventually became *Heller's* individualist theory.

Within ten years of its publication, two more law journal articles appeared in support of this position; in the 1970s, six more were published; in the 1980s, 21 were published in law journals; in the 1990s, 58, with many more since. During these four decades, a similar number of articles was published on the opposing side, but by now this blizzard of writing on the Second Amendment had transformed agreed-upon meaning into a debate where both sides seemed equally legitimate—as if supporters of "scientific creationism" had succeeded in flooding science journals with articles about evolution to produce an apparent academic stalemate between seemingly equivalent dueling scientific interpretations.

If law journal writing didn't matter, then student control wouldn't either. But law reviews do matter. They shape national policy debates, legislatures, presidents, and, in this case, judges. It is of no small importance that many of President [George W.] Bush's unprecedentedly expansive claims to presidential power trace back to a 1996 law review article written by law professor and administration lawyer John Yoo. And Scalia's majority opinion in *Heller* is laced with, and built upon, this law journal writing, replete as it is with "law office history."

Manufactured Scholarship

In the world of law journals, publication decisions by student editors are too often based on factors like author reputation, affiliation with the institution publishing the journal, sheer length, and whether the submission seems unusual or unorthodox. No one with control over publication is in a position to know whether the author knows what has already been written on the subject, whether the argument is legitimate, the history sound. Yes, additional articles can be published pointing out such flaws, but this negates the very idea of scholarly writing, where vetting must occur before publication, for the very reason that publication is itself the most important act legitimating an idea.

Gun rights enthusiasts, eager to establish an "originalist" constitutional pedigree for their developing political movement, used student-run law reviews to craft and burnish an idea that, until now, found no traction in the courts. Constitutional doctrine is properly ever-evolving, but that evolution ought not to be shaped by manufactured provenance masquerading as scholarship.

> "Does the preface [of the Second
> Amendment] fit with an operative
> clause that creates an individual right
> to keep and bear arms? It fits perfectly."

The Second Amendment Applies to Individuals, Not Just Militias

Antonin Scalia

Antonin Scalia is a justice of the United States Supreme Court. In the following majority opinion, he argues that the original purpose of the Second Amendment at the time of the creation of the Constitution was to ensure a right for individuals to defend against tyrannical injustice. He says, therefore, that the Second Amendment's mention of militias is secondary to its assurance of the right to self-defense. He concludes that the Second Amendment protects an individual right to bear arms, not just the maintenance of militias.

As you read, consider the following questions:

1. Who is Dick Heller, according to Scalia?
2. Why does the author say we start with a presumption that the Second Amendment right is exercised individually?

Antonin Scalia, "District of Colubmia v. Heller," law.cornell.edu, no. 07-290, June 26, 2008. Supreme Court of the United States.

3. According to Scalia, why did colonists during the 1760s and 1770s invoke their rights as Englishmen to bear arms?

We consider whether a District of Columbia [D.C.] prohibition on the possession of usable handguns in the home violates the Second Amendment to the Constitution.

The District of Columbia generally prohibits the possession of handguns. It is a crime to carry an unregistered firearm, and the registration of handguns is prohibited. Wholly apart from that prohibition, no person may carry a handgun without a license, but the chief of police may issue licenses for 1-year periods. District of Columbia law also requires residents to keep their lawfully owned firearms, such as registered long guns, "unloaded and dis[as]sembled or bound by a trigger lock or similar device" unless they are located in a place of business or are being used for lawful recreational activities.

Respondent Dick Heller is a D.C. special police officer authorized to carry a handgun while on duty at the Federal Judicial Center. He applied for a registration certificate for a handgun that he wished to keep at home, but the District refused. He thereafter filed a lawsuit in the Federal District Court for the District of Columbia seeking, on Second Amendment grounds, to enjoin the city from enforcing the bar on the registration of handguns, the licensing requirement insofar as it prohibits the carrying of a firearm in the home without a license, and the trigger-lock requirement insofar as it prohibits the use of "functional firearms within the home." The District Court dismissed respondent's complaint. The Court of Appeals for the District of Columbia Circuit, construing his complaint as seeking the right to render a firearm operable and carry it about his home in that condition only when necessary for self-defense, reversed, see *Parker v. District of Columbia*. It held that the Second Amendment protects an individual right to possess firearms and that the city's total ban on handguns, as well as its requirement that firearms in the home be kept nonfunctional even when necessary for self-defense, violated that right. . . . The Court of Appeals directed the District Court to enter summary judgment for respondent.

We granted certiorari [a grant of Supreme Court review].

The Meaning of the Second Amendment

We turn first to the meaning of the Second Amendment.

The Second Amendment provides: "A well regulated Militia, being necessary to the security of a free State, the right of the people to keep and bear Arms, shall not be infringed."[1] In interpreting this text, we are guided by the principle that "[t]he Constitution was written to be understood by the voters; its words and phrases were used in their normal and ordinary meaning as distinguished from technical meaning." Normal meaning may of course include an idiomatic meaning, but it excludes secret or technical meanings that would not have been known to ordinary citizens in the founding generation.

The two sides in this case have set out very different interpretations of the Amendment. Petitioners and today's dissenting Justices believe that it protects only the right to possess and carry a firearm in connection with militia service. Respondent argues that it protects an individual right to possess a firearm unconnected with service in a militia, and to use that arm for traditionally lawful purposes, such as self-defense within the home.

The Second Amendment is naturally divided into two parts: its prefatory clause and its operative clause. The former does not limit the latter grammatically, but rather announces a purpose. The Amendment could be rephrased, "Because a well regulated Militia is necessary to the security of a free State, the right of the people to keep and bear Arms shall not be infringed." Although this structure of the Second Amendment is unique in our Constitution, other legal documents of the founding era, particularly individual-rights provisions of state constitutions, commonly included a prefatory statement of purpose.

Logic demands that there be a link between the stated purpose and the command. The Second Amendment would be nonsensical if it read, "A well regulated Militia, being necessary to the security of a free State, the right of the people to petition for redress of grievances shall not be infringed." That requirement of logical connection may cause a prefatory clause to resolve an ambiguity in the operative clause ("The separation of church and state being an important objective, the teachings of canons shall have no place in our jurisprudence." The preface makes clear that the operative clause refers not to canons of interpretation but to clergymen.) But apart from that clarifying function, a prefatory clause does not limit or expand the scope of the operative clause. Therefore, while we will begin our textual analysis with the operative clause, we will return to the prefatory clause to ensure that our reading of the operative clause is consistent with the announced purpose.

"Right of the People"

The first salient feature of the operative clause is that it codifies a "right of the people." The unamended Constitution and the Bill of Rights use the phrase "right of the people" two other times, in the First Amendment's Assembly-and-Petition Clause and in the Fourth Amendment's Search-and-Seizure Clause. The Ninth Amendment uses very similar terminology ("The enumeration in the Constitution, of certain rights, shall not be construed to deny or disparage others retained by the people"). All three of these instances unambiguously refer to individual rights, not "collective" rights, or rights that may be exercised only through participation in some corporate body.

Three provisions of the Constitution refer to "the people" in a context other than "rights"—the famous preamble ("We the people"), §2 of Article I (providing that "the people" will choose members of the House), and the Tenth Amendment (providing that those powers not given the Federal Government remain with "the States" or "the people"). Those provisions arguably refer to "the people" acting collectively—but they deal with the exercise or reservation of powers, not rights. Nowhere else in the Constitution does a "right" attributed to "the people" refer to anything other than an individual right. . . .

We start therefore with a strong presumption that the Second Amendment right is exercised individually and belongs to all Americans. . . .

The Historical Background

Putting all of these textual elements together, we find that they guarantee the individual right to possess and carry weapons in case of confrontation. This meaning is strongly confirmed by the historical background of the Second Amendment. We look to this because it has always been widely understood that the Second Amendment, like the First and Fourth Amendments, codified a *pre-existing* right. The very text of the Second Amendment implicitly recognizes the pre-existence of the right and declares only that it "shall not be infringed." As we said in *United States v. Cruikshank* (1876), "[t]his is not a right granted by the Constitution. Neither is it in any manner dependent upon that instrument for its existence. The Second Amendment declares that it shall not be infringed. . . . "

Between the Restoration [1660 in England] and the Glorious Revolution [1688], the Stuart Kings Charles II and James II succeeded in using select militias loyal to them to suppress political dissidents, in part by disarming their opponents. Under the auspices of the 1671 Game Act, for example, the Catholic James II had ordered general disarmaments of regions home to his Protestant enemies. These experiences caused Englishmen to be extremely wary of concentrated military forces run by the state and to be jealous of their arms. They accordingly obtained an assurance from William and Mary, in the Declaration of Right (which was codified as the English Bill of Rights), that Protestants would never be disarmed: "That the subjects which are Protestants may have arms for their defense suitable to their conditions and as allowed by law." This right has long been understood to be the predecessor to our Second Amendment. It was clearly an individual right, having nothing whatever to do with service in a militia. To be sure, it was an individual right not available to the whole population, given that it was restricted to Protestants, and like all written English rights it was held only against the Crown, not Parliament. But it was secured to them as individuals, according to "libertarian political principles," not as members of a fighting force. . . .

And, of course, what the Stuarts had tried to do to their political enemies, George III had tried to do to the colonists [at the time of the American Revolution]. In the tumultuous decades of the 1760's and 1770's, the Crown began to disarm the inhabitants of the most rebellious areas. That provoked polemical reactions by Americans invoking their rights as Englishmen to keep arms. A New York article of April 1769 said that "[i]t is a natural right which the people have reserved to themselves, confirmed by the Bill of Rights, to keep arms for their own defence." . . .

There seems to us no doubt, on the basis of both text and history, that the Second Amendment conferred an individual right to keep and bear arms. Of course the right was not unlimited, just as the First Amendment's right of free speech was not. Thus, we do not read the Second Amendment to protect the right of citizens to carry arms for *any sort* of confrontation, just as we do not read the First Amendment to protect the right of citizens to speak for *any purpose*. Before turning to limitations upon the individual right, however, we must determine whether the prefatory clause of the Second Amendment comports with our interpretation of the operative clause.

Prefatory Clause

The prefatory clause reads: "A well regulated Militia, being necessary to the security of a free State. . . ."

Young America and the Right to Guns

The America of the founding era was indeed a place where a gun was a common day-to-day accoutrement of life, and a tool vital for both civic and personal purposes. Young America already had a strong tradition of guns as tools for protection, recreation, rebellion, and food. It was a country fresh out of a revolution in which widespread possession of, and some skill in using, weapons was central to victory. It remembered the indignities and dangers of General Thomas Gage's attempts to disarm the citizens of Boston in 1775.

The United States was a country whose citizens had a right—which the government could not abrogate—to possess arms for their personal use. That should have been unsurprising and obvious. And it was.

Brian Doherty, Gun Control on Trial:
Inside the Supreme Court Battle over the
Second Amendment, *2008.*

"Well-Regulated Militia." In *United States v. Miller* (1939), we explained that "the Militia comprised all males physically capable of acting in concert for the common defense." That definition comports with founding-era sources. . . .

Petitioners take a seemingly narrower view of the militia, stating that "[m]ilitias are the state- and congressionally-regulated military forces described in the Militia Clauses." Although we agree with petitioners' interpretive assumption that "militia" means the same thing in Article I and the Second Amendment, we believe that petitioners identify the wrong thing, namely, the organized militia. Unlike armies and navies, which Congress is given the power to create, the militia is assumed by Article I already to be *in existence.* Congress is given the power to "provide for calling forth the militia," §8, cl. 15; and the power not to create, but to "organiz[e]" it—and not to organize "a" militia, which is what one would expect if the militia were to be a federal creation, but to organize "the" militia, connoting a body already in existence. This is fully consistent with the ordinary definition of the militia as all able-bodied men. From that pool, Congress has plenary power to organize the units that will make up an effective fighting force. That is what Congress did in the first militia Act, which specified that "each and every free, able-bodied white male citizen of the respective states, resident therein, who is or shall be of the age of eighteen years, and under the age of forty-five years (except as is herein after excepted) shall severally and respectively be enrolled in the militia." To be sure, Congress need not conscript every able-bodied man into the militia, because nothing in Article I suggests that in exercising its power to organize, discipline, and arm the militia, Congress must focus upon the entire body. Although the militia consists of all able-bodied men, the federally organized militia may consist of a subset of them.

Finally, the adjective "well-regulated" implies nothing more than the imposition of proper discipline and training. . . .

The Clauses Fit

We reach the question, then: Does the preface fit with an operative clause that creates an individual right to keep and bear arms? It fits perfectly, once one knows the history that the founding generation knew and that we have described above. That history showed that the way tyrants had eliminated a militia consisting of all the able-bodied men was not by banning the militia but simply by taking away the people's arms, enabling a select militia or standing army to suppress political opponents. This is what had occurred in England that prompted codification of the right to have arms in the English Bill of Rights.

The debate with respect to the right to keep and bear arms, as with other guarantees in the Bill of Rights, was not over whether it was desirable (all agreed that it was) but over whether it needed to be codified in the Constitution. During the 1788 ratification debates, the fear that the federal government would disarm the people in order to impose rule through a standing army or select militia was pervasive in Antifederalist rhetoric [the Antifederalists opposed a strong central government]. John Smilie, for example, worried not only that Congress's "command of the militia" could be used to create a "select militia," or to have "no militia at all," but also, as a separate concern, that "[w]hen a select militia is formed; the people in general may be disarmed." Federalists responded that because Congress was given no power to abridge the ancient right of individuals to keep and bear arms, such a force could never oppress the people. It was understood across the political spectrum that the right helped to secure the ideal of a citizen militia, which might be necessary to oppose an oppressive military force if the constitutional order broke down.

It is therefore entirely sensible that the Second Amendment's prefatory clause announces the purpose for which the right was codified: to prevent elimination of the militia. The prefatory clause does not suggest that preserving the militia was the only reason Americans valued the ancient right; most undoubtedly they thought it even more important for self-defense and hunting. But the threat that the new Federal Government would destroy the citizens' militia by taking away their arms was the reason that right—unlike some other English rights—was codified in a written Constitution. Justice [Stephen] Breyer's assertion that individual self-defense is merely a "subsidiary interest" of the right to keep and bear arms, is profoundly mistaken. He bases that assertion solely upon the prologue—but that can only show that self-defense had little to do with the right's *codification*; it was the *central component* of the right itself.

Note

1. The part beginning "A well regulated. . ." is known as the preface, or the prefatory clause. The part beginning with "the right of the people" is called the operative clause.

> "The . . . Second Amendment was . . .
> a civic right that guaranteed that
> citizens would be able to keep and bear
> those arms needed to meet their legal
> obligation to participate in a well-
> regulated militia."

The Second Amendment Guaranteed a Civic Right to Be Part of the State Militia

Saul Cornell

Saul Cornell is a professor of American history at Fordham University in New York City. In the following viewpoint he argues that both sides in the gun control debate are wrong. Pro-gun forces are incorrect in claiming that the Second Amendment provides an individual right, he says. He also says that anti-gun forces are incorrect in claiming it provides only a collective right. Instead, he argues, the Second Amendment originally provided a civic right to keep and bear a gun in order to fulfill service in a "well-regulated" militia.

As you read, consider the following questions:

1. How does Cornell say that the minutemen captured the

original Constitutional ideal of the Second Amendment?

2. According to the author, when and how did the fear that the individual right of self-defense was threatened come into being?

3. Why does Cornell believe that the modern gun control movement's embrace of the collective rights theory of the Second Amendment is laden with irony?

Whipping the crowd into a frenzy at the National Rifle Association annual convention, Charlton Heston, the group's charismatic president, raised an antique musket above his head and challenged gun control proponents to pry his weapon from his "cold, dead hands." This defiant gesture, repeated on numerous occasions by the chisel-jawed actor known for his portrayals of key figures in history, has become a powerful symbol in America's bitter debate over the right to bear arms. To dramatize his rebellious stance, Heston did not wave a modern assault rifle, but a Revolutionary-era musket, an iconic symbol that adorns pro-gun Web sites, tee shirts, and bumper stickers.

The Original Meaning

History is at the very heart of the rancorous debate over guns in America, and no issue is more controversial than the original meaning of the Second Amendment. Partisans of gun rights argue that the Second Amendment protects an individual right to keep and bear arms for self-defense, recreation, and, if necessary, to take up arms against their government. Gun control advocates also claim to have history on their side and maintain with equal vigor that the Second Amendment simply protects a collective right of the states. Both sides have the history wrong.

The original understanding of the Second Amendment was neither an individual right of self-defense nor a collective right of the states, but rather a civic right that guaranteed that citizens would be able to keep and bear those arms needed to meet their legal obligation to participate in a well-regulated militia. Nothing better captured this constitutional ideal than the minuteman. Citizens had a legal obligation to outfit themselves with a musket at their own expense and were expected to turn out at a minute's notice to defend their community, state, and eventually their nation. The minuteman ideal was far less individualistic than most gun rights people assume, and far more martial in spirit than most gun control advocates realize.

Although each side in the modern debate claims to be faithful to the historical Second Amendment, a restoration of its original meaning, re-creating the world of the minuteman, would be a nightmare that neither side would welcome. It would certainly involve more intrusive gun regulation, not less. Proponents of gun rights would not relish the idea of mandatory gun registration, nor would they be eager to welcome government officials into their homes to inspect privately owned weapons, as they did in Revolutionary days. Gun control advocates might blanch at the notion that all Americans would be required to receive firearms training and would certainly look askance at the idea of requiring all able-bodied citizens to purchase their own military-style assault weapons. Yet if the civic right to bear arms of the Founding were reintroduced, this is exactly what citizens would be obligated to do. A restoration of the original understanding of the Second Amendment would require all these measures and much more.

Liberty and Regulation

Most Americans no longer live in the small rural communities that nurtured the minuteman ideal. Regulation in modern America is typically seen as antithetical to rights. The opposite was the case for the colonists, who believed that liberty without regulation was anarchy. Without government regulation there would have been no minutemen to muster on the town greens at Lexington and Concord. The state's coercive authority over citizens could be significant. Failure to appear properly armed at a muster resulted in stiff penalties, and government kept close tabs on the weapons citizens owned to meet this vital public obligation. Although ardent in their love of freedom, Americans feared anarchy as much as they dreaded tyranny. An armed body of citizens unregulated by law was a mob, not a militia. The golden mean between the two extremes of anarchy and tyranny was the idea of well-regulated liberty, and nothing better captured this ideal than the militia.

The militia statutes each colony enacted tell only part of the story of how this vital institution was enmeshed in the everyday lives of most colonists. If history taught Americans any lesson, it was that a standing army of professional soldiers presented a perpetual threat to freedom. A well-regulated militia was the only form of defense compatible with liberty. Only when the role of citizen and soldier were united could freedom be preserved. The militia not only protected Americans from external threats such as hostile Indians and rival European powers, but in an era before organized police forces it also provided the only means to protect communities from civil unrest. Before the rise of modern political parties, militia units provided an essential means for organizing citizens for political action. Muster days were important festive occasions that drew citizens together for celebration and revelry.

The Americans who enshrined the right to bear arms in the first state constitutions were haunted by a fear of disarmament, but this fear was quite different than the fears of gun confiscation that cloud contemporary debates over firearms. The Concord minuteman who fired the shots heard round the world had been mustered on that fateful day to prevent British regular troops from confiscating the militia's powder and arms. The first statements of the right to bear arms in American constitutional law were clearly aimed at protecting the militia against the danger of being disarmed by the government, not at protecting individual citizens' right of personal self-defense.

Personal Self-Defense

Although most eighteenth-century Americans did not fear that
the individual right of self-defense might be threatened, this
fear did eventually take hold decades after Americans wrote
their first constitutions. In the early nineteenth century some
Americans did come to believe this right was under assault.
The threat these Americans felt did not come from a despotic
monarch or an omnipotent Parliament, but from their own state
legislatures. A profound shift in the character of firearms regulation occurred in the early decades of the nineteenth century. In
response to widespread fears that handguns and bowie knives
posed a serious threat to social stability, legislatures enacted the
first comprehensive laws prohibiting handguns and other concealed weapons. Then, as now, the enactment of gun control laws
prompted a backlash that led to an intensified commitment to
gun rights. One of the many embarrassing truths about the debate over the right to bear arms that neither side wishes to admit
is that gun rights ideology is the illegitimate and spurned child
of gun control. These early efforts at gun control spawned the
first legal challenges to these types of laws premised on the idea
of a constitutional right to bear arms for individual self-defense.
While most courts upheld gun control laws and continued to assert a civic conception of the right to bear arms, a few courts
embraced the new ideology of gun rights. One of the principal
confusions in the modern debate over gun regulation, the blurring of the distinction between the constitutional right to bear
arms for public defense and the individual right to bear a gun
in self-defense, crystallized in the Jacksonian era. Public debate
over gun control has stumbled over this issue ever since.

If the debate over the right to bear arms had remained simply
a matter of state constitutional law, then the story would be quite
straightforward: the growth of an individual rights view and its
ongoing struggle against the original civic vision of arms bearing. The only problem with this story is that it tells us nothing
about the Second Amendment, which emerged out of the divi-

sive struggle between Federalists [who supported greater federal power] and Anti-Federalists [who supported states rights] over the new Constitution. To understand this history one must deal with the way that this right became embroiled in the bitter debate over federalism. No issue in early American constitutional law was more contentious than the battle between proponents of states' rights and supporters of national power. While the language of the provision on arms bearing that Congress drafted, which eventually became the Second Amendment, was closer in spirit to the civic model embodied in the first state constitutions, Anti-Federalists and their Jeffersonian heirs came to interpret the Second Amendment within an evolving theory of states' rights. The right to bear arms in a well-regulated militia controlled by the states would provide the ultimate check on federal power if such power ran amok. The original Anti-Federalist understanding of the Second Amendment was revolutionary, assigning to the state militias the awesome power to resist federal authority by force of arms.

The Fourteenth Amendment

The modern gun control movement's embrace of the collective rights theory of the Second Amendment is laden with irony. Contemporary gun control theory rests on a strong commitment to a powerful federal regulatory state. Few partisans of this theory realize that its constitutional roots may be found in a radical states' rights ideology that advanced a revolutionary challenge to federal power. Of course the version of states' rights that lies at the heart of modern gun control ideology only faintly resembles its radical ancestor. To understand how states' rights theory was drained of its revolutionary potential we must examine the pivotal role that the Civil War and Reconstruction played in transforming the meaning of the Second Amendment. The foundation for the modern collective rights theory was forged in the carnage of the Reconstruction era [the post–Civil War period].

Regulation and the Founding Fathers

The thing one has to appreciate in trying to understand the history of the Second Amendment is that we've had gun regulation as long as there have been guns in America. The Founding Fathers were not opposed to the idea of regulation. In fact, their view of liberty was something that they would have described as "well-regulated liberty." The idea of regulation, the idea of reasonable government regulation, was absolutely essential to the way they understood liberty. In fact, in their view, if you didn't have regulation, you had anarchy. Next to tyranny, anarchy was the thing they feared most. So it's really almost impossible to understand the Founding Fathers and their world view, including their views of guns, without understanding that they were strongly committed to the idea of regulation.

Saul Cornell, interviewed by BuzzFlash,
"'The Second Amendment Doesn't Prohibit
Gun Regulation—It in Fact Compels
It,' According to Professor Saul Cornell,"
September 4, 2006. http://blog.buzzflash.com.

The evolution of modern Second Amendment theory is closely bound up with the debate over the Fourteenth Amendment [which applied the Bill of Rights to the states as well as the federal government]. Republican framers of the Fourteenth Amendment intended to give the federal government the power to incorporate the fundamental liberties protected by the Bill of Rights. According to incorporation theory, Congress and the courts would be given the authority to guard basic liberties, including the right to bear arms. Democrats argued against incorporation and claimed that the Second Amendment was a right of the states, not a right of citizens. In the Democrats' narrow states' rights theory, the amendment did no more than restrain Congress from disarming the state militias. Ultimately, the courts rejected the Republican theory of incorporation and embraced the Democratic states' rights theory of the Second Amendment.

The transformation of this late nineteenth-century states' rights theory into the modern collective rights theory was accomplished early in the twentieth century as judges, lawyers, and reformers grappled with the new problems posed by organized crime and gun violence. If the Second Amendment was merely a right of the states designed to prevent federal disarmament of the state militias, then, gun control proponents claimed, it posed no barrier to state or federal gun control laws. One additional change in American law and society facilitated the final transformation of the Second Amendment into a collective right: Congress replaced the Founding era's universal militia with the modern National Guard. Ordinary citizens could no longer make a claim to keep and bear private arms to meet their public obligation to participate in the militia. The connection between arms bearing and civic participation had been effectively severed. Only the participants in legally sanctioned military organizations could now make Second Amendment claims.

The Civic Conception

Neither of the two modern theories that have defined public debate over the right to bear arms is faithful to the original understanding of this provision of the Bill of Rights. Previous scholarship on this history has been warped by the ideological needs of the modern debate over gun control. Only by casting aside the ideology of gun rights and gun control can one discern the real and previously hidden history of the great American gun debate. While no scholar writing about this contentious issue can claim to be completely above the fray or entirely neutral, it is possible to approach this issue in a rigorous and balanced manner, focusing on the hopes and fears that drove earlier generations of Americans to venerate the right to bear arms and not confusing these debates with the modern conflict over gun control.

One need not deny gun rights advocates and gun control proponents their history. While each side attacks the other for being a recent invention, the truth is that both sides have a rich history that has much to teach anyone interested in the role of guns in American society. While these opposing theories have deep roots in American history, there is little evidence that either theory was part of the original civic understanding that guided the framers of America's first constitutions. The individual rights and collective rights theories were products of later struggles in American history. Individual rights theory was born in the Jacksonian era [1820s and 1830s] as a response to America's first efforts at gun control. Collective rights theory emerged slowly at the end of Reconstruction and only crystallized in its modern form in the early twentieth century. The one theory absent from current debate over the Second Amendment is the original civic interpretation. The virtual extinction of this conception was not inevitable but was a product of a long and complex history. Although the story of the decline of the civic conception of the right to bear arms has never been told, this history is vital to understanding our current predicament over guns in American society.

The tangled history of the struggle to define the right to bear arms ought to serve as a cautionary warning to both sides in this debate. If history seems to provide clear and unambiguous support for ones' ideological preferences in the great American gun debate, then the history is likely wrong. While history may not help us chart a clear path toward a solution to America's bitter conflict over the role of guns in American society, some appreciation for how we have arrived at our current deadlock is an important first step to moving forward in this debate.

> "The National Defense Act of 1916 . . .
> expanded the Guard's role and
> guaranteed the State militias' status as
> the Army's primary reserve force."

The National Guard Is a Constitutional Militia

Army National Guard

The Army National Guard is a reserve military force composed of state National Guard militia members. The following viewpoint presents and interprets the portions of the US Constitution that provide for a militia. It also lists the most important laws that have established and provided for a National Guard. It suggests that the National Guard is an outgrowth of the constitutional militia and fulfills the vision of the Founding Fathers.

As you read, consider the following questions:

1. What is the armies clause in the Constitution, and what does it provide for, according to the author?
2. How does the Army National Guard say that the militia concept was put to the test in the War of 1812?
3. How did the Total Force Policy of 1973 respond to the Vietnam War, according to the author?

"Legal Basis of the National Guard," Army National Guard, 2009.

The National Guard's charter is the Constitution of the United States. Article I, Section 8 of the U.S. Constitution contains a series of "militia clauses," vesting distinct authority and responsibilities in the federal government and the state governments. These clauses and follow-on legislation have sculpted the Guard as you see it today. Here are summaries that will help you understand how the Guard came to be what it is today.

The Constitution and Militias

Article I, Section 8; Clause 15 . . . provides that the Congress has three constitutional grounds for calling up the militia—"to execute the laws of the Union, suppress insurrection and repel invasions." All three standards appear to be applicable only to the Territory of the United States.

Article I, Section 8; Clause 16 . . . gives Congress the power "to provide for organizing, arming and disciplining the militia, and for governing such part of them as may be employed in the service of the United States." That same clause specifically reserves to the States the authority to establish a state-based militia, to appoint the officers and to train the militia according to the discipline prescribed by the Congress. As written, the clause seeks to limit federal power over State militias during peacetime.

The Armies Clause

"Congress may declare war, raise and support armies . . . "

The "armies clause" in Article I, Section 8, conferred on Congress the power to provide for the common defense of the United States, declare war, raise and support armies, and make rules for the "government and regulation of the land and naval forces." The Congress also was granted authority to make all laws "necessary and proper" for carrying out such powers. Under this provision, congressional power over the National Guard appears to be far-reaching. . . .

Article I, Section 10 provides that no state, without the consent of the Congress, shall keep troops or ships of war in time of peace, or engage in war unless actually invaded. Be sure to see the Second Amendment for more about this.

The Second Amendment

" . . . A well-regulated militia [is] necessary to the security of a free State," and " . . . the right of the people to keep and bear arms shall not be infringed."

The Second Amendment qualified Article I, Section 10 by ensuring that the federal government could not disarm the state militias. One part of the Bill of Rights, insisted on by the anti-federalists, states, "A well-regulated militia, being necessary to the security of a free State, the right of the people to keep and bear arms shall not be infringed." . . .

Article IV, Section 4 provides that the federal government "shall guarantee to every State in this Union a republican form of government," and shall protect each of the States against invasion. At State request, the federal government was to protect the States "against domestic violence." Through these provisions, the potential for both cooperative Federalism and for tension between the "militia" and the "army" clauses was built into the Constitution. . . .

Article II, Section 2 places all forces, including the militia when in federal service, under the control of the executive branch by making the president Commander-in-Chief. . . .

Article I, Section 8 gave the ultimate control to the Congress, by granting it the sole power to collect taxes to pay for the military, to declare war and to employ the militia for common purposes of internal security. Existing State militias could be maintained, although troops could be called into national service. But the founding fathers moderated that authority by leaving the individual States with the explicit responsibility for appointing officers and for supervising peacetime training of the citizen-soldiers. . . .

Laws and Militias

The Militia Act of 1792 subsequently expanded federal policy and clarified the role of the militia. It required all able-bodied men aged 18 to 45 to serve, to be armed, to be equipped at their own expense and to participate in annual musters. The 1792 act established the idea of organizing these militia forces into standard divisions, brigades, regiments, battalions and companies, as directed by the State legislatures. . . .

For the 111 years that the Militia Act of 1792 remained in effect, it defined the position of the militia in relation to the federal government. The War of 1812 tested this unique American defense establishment. To fight the War of 1812, the republic formed a small regular military and trained it to protect the frontiers and coastlines. Although it performed poorly in the offensive against Canada, the small force of regulars backed by a well-armed militia, accomplished its defensive mission well. Generals like Andrew Jackson proved, just as they had in the Revolution, that regulars and militia could be effective when employed as a team. . . .

Posse Comitatus

In 1867, the Congress suspended the southern states' right to organize their militias until a state was firmly under the control of an acceptable government. The U.S. Army was used to enforce martial law in the South during Reconstruction. Expansion of the military's role in domestic life, however, did not occur without debate or response. Reaction to the use of the Army in suppressing labor unrest in the North and guarding polls in the South during the 1876 election led to congressional enactment of the Posse Comitatus Act in 1878. Designed to limit the president's use of military forces in peacetime, this statute provided that: " . . . it shall not be lawful to employ any part of the Army of the United States . . . for the purpose of executing the laws, except on such cases and under such circumstances as such employment of said force may be expressly authorized by the Constitution or by any act of Congress . . . "

What Is the National Guard?

The National Guard serves both state and federal governments. The difference between the Guard and other branches is that while Guard units are combat-trained and can be deployed overseas, they are just as likely to serve in their home communities—training just one weekend per month, and one two-week period each year.

During local emergencies, Guard units assist residents endangered by storms, floods, fires and other disasters. Guard companies deployed overseas may see combat, but are often found building schools and hospitals, training local peace-keepers or teaching local farmers more efficient techniques and better uses of their land.

"What Is the Guard?"
www.nationalguard.com.

The Rise of the National Guard

Concern over the militia's new domestic role also led the States to reexamine their need for a well-equipped and trained militia, and between 1881 and 1892, every state revised the military code to provide for an organized force. Most changed the name of their militias to the National Guard, following New York's example. . . .

Between 1903 and the 1920's, legislation was enacted that strengthened the Army National Guard as a component of the national defense force. The Dick Act of 1903 replaced the 1792 Militia Act and affirmed the National Guard as the Army's primary organized reserve. . . .

The National Defense Act of 1916 further expanded the Guard's role and guaranteed the State militias' status as the

Army's primary reserve force. Furthermore, the law mandated use of the term "National Guard" for that force. Moreover, the President was given authority, in case of war or national emergency, to mobilize the National Guard for the duration of the emergency. The number of yearly drills increased from 24 to 48 and annual training from five to 15 days. Drill pay was authorized for the first time. . . .

The National Defense Act Amendments of 1920 established that the chief of the Militia Bureau (later the National Guard Bureau) would be a National Guard officer, that National Guard officers would be assigned to the general staff and that the divisions, as used by the Guard in World War I, would be reorganized. . . .

The National Guard Mobilization Act of 1933 made the National Guard of the United States a component of the Army at all times, which could be ordered into active federal service by the President whenever Congress declared a national emergency. . . .

Following the experience of fighting an unpopular war in Vietnam, the 1973 Total Force Policy was designed to involve a large portion of the American public by mobilizing the National Guard from its thousands of locations throughout the United States when needed. The Total Force Policy required that all active and reserve military organizations of the United States be treated as a single integrated force. A related benefit of this approach is to permit elected officials to have a better sense of public support or opposition to any major military operation. This policy echoes the original intentions of the founding fathers for a small standing army complemented by citizen-soldiers.

"Building on a strong U.S. militia tradition, today's State Defense Forces offer a vital force multiplier and homeland security resource."

State Defense Forces Are Vital Constitutional Militias

James Carafano and Jessica Zuckerman

James Carafano is director of the Douglas and Sarah Allison Center for Foreign Policy Studies at the Heritage Foundation, a conservative Washington, D.C., policy research organization; Jessica Zuckerman is a research assistant at the foundation. In the following viewpoint they argue that State Defense Forces (SDFs) can be an important part of state security and disaster response. The authors argue that SDFs are constitutional. They also argue that SDFs can respond quickly to local disasters, especially when many National Guard troops are deployed overseas. The authors conclude that SDFs should be more widely used, more widely recognized, and better funded and equipped.

As you read, consider the following questions:

1. According to the authors, how many states and territories have modern militas, and what was their force strength as of 2005?

2. What two advantages do SDFs have because of their state service status, according to Carafano and Zuckerman?

3. What do the authors say is one of the greatest challenges facing SDFs?

S ince the founding of the United States of America, local militias have played an important role in its defense and security. Bolstered by the Founding Fathers' concerns about maintaining a large standing army and preserved within the Constitution, the concept of the citizen soldier has since become ingrained in American culture and government.

The Value of SDFs

Currently, 23 states and territories have modern militias. As of 2005, these militias had a force strength of approximately 14,000 individuals nationwide. Most commonly known as State Defense Forces (SDFs) or state militias, these forces are distinct from the Reserves and the National Guard in that they serve no federal function. In times of both war and peace, SDFs remain solely under the control of their governors, allowing the governors to deploy them easily and readily in the event of a natural or man-made disaster.

Building on a strong U.S. militia tradition, today's State Defense Forces offer a vital force multiplier and homeland security resource for governors throughout the nation. SDFs can greatly fortify homeland security efforts in the states by serving as emergency response and recovery forces. Consequently, state leaders should make strengthening existing SDFs a priority, while encouraging their creation in states that do not yet have SDFs, especially in states at high risk of a natural or man-made disaster. . . .

At present, 23 states and territories have SDFs, and their estimated force strength totaled 14,000 members as of 2005. Authorized under federal statute Title 32 of the U.S. Code, SDFs are entirely under state control—unlike the National Guard—both in peace and otherwise. Hence, while the National Guard is a dual-apportioned force that can be called to federal service under Title 10 or remain a state force under Title 32, State Defense Forces serve solely as Title 32 forces.

This status gives SDFs two important advantages. First, SDFs are continually stationed within their respective states and can be called up quickly and easily in times of need. Such a capability is particularly important when catastrophic disasters overwhelm local first responders and federal forces can take up to 72 hours to respond. Second, SDFs are exempt from the restrictions of the Posse Comitatus Act, which prohibits federal military forces from engaging in domestic law enforcement activities within the United States. While the Posse Comitatus Act has never proven a major obstacle to deploying federal forces for domestic emergency response, SDFs permit a state military response uninhibited by legal obstacles.

Each SDF is under the control of its respective governor through the state's military department. The Adjutant General [TAG], the state's senior military commander and a member of the governor's cabinet, commands the SDF on behalf of the governor. As SDF commander, TAG is responsible for all training, equipment allocation, and decisions regarding the SDF's strength, activity, and mission. The Adjutant General is also the commander of the state's National Guard units and often directs state emergency response. Through TAGs, SDFs can easily coordinate with other key components of the state emergency response.

Despite its recognition in federal statute, creation of a State Defense Force remains at the discretion of each state governor, and 28 states have chosen not to create such forces. Creation of SDFs has met resistance from TAGs and the National Guard Bureau due to concerns over turf, costs, and even arming SDF members. However, such objections make little sense given that SDFs are entirely volunteer organizations and offer the states a vital, low-cost force multiplier. Members are not paid for training, only some states compensate them for active duty, and SDFs generally have little equipment. For example, in 2002 alone, the Georgia State Guard reportedly saved the state of Georgia $1.5 million by providing 1,797 days of operational service to the state. In all, the state-apportioned status, organizational structure, and low-cost burden of SDFs make them a vital and practical resource for the states.

State Defense Forces Post-9/11

Only months before 9/11, the U.S. Commission on National Security/21st Century (the Hart-Rudman Commission) suggested making homeland security the primary mission of the National Guard. However, after September 11, 2001, National Guard deployments reached their highest level since the Korean War. This was understandably troubling to many state leaders given that "[g]overnors have the greatest responsibility for managing consequences of attacks," but "[t]hey have the fewest resources with which to do it . . . only the state police and the National Guard to provide for law and order." In recent years, the high levels of National Guard deployment largely removed this resource from numerous states. Even in the states where National Guard forces remain present, the Guard is maintaining only about 62 percent of its equipment on hand for the states because of overseas deployments. This has left some governors with just state police units to help to maintain security and facilitate emergency response. In addition, an emergency, particularly a catastrophic disaster, could quickly overwhelm state police and other first responders. If National Guard forces are unavailable because they are deployed elsewhere, then the state could rely on its SDF, if it has one, to reinforce police and first responders. While largely underdeveloped and underresourced, SDFs can fill this gap in state homeland security capabilities, giving governors a valuable force multiplier.

In recent years, State Defense Forces have proven vital to homeland security and emergency response efforts. For exam-

Total Active Strength of State Defense Forces in Selected States, as of January 2010

Alabama	200+
Georgia	800
Indiana	200+
Maryland	200+
Michigan	100–200
Mississippi	200+
New Mexico	60–80
Ohio	101–200
Oregon	100–200
Tennessee	489
Texas	1,750
Vermont	200+
Virginia	1,050

TAKEN FROM: James Carafano and Jessica Zuckerman, "Backgrounder No. 2474: Appendix B," *Heritage Foundation*, October 8, 2010, p.14. http://thf_media.s3.amazonaws.com/2010/pdf/bg2474.pdf.

ple, after 9/11, the New York Guard, New York Naval Militia, and New Jersey Naval Militia were activated to assist in response measures, recovery efforts, and critical infrastructure security. An estimated 2,274 SDF personnel participated in support of recovery efforts after Hurricane Katrina. SDF personnel were activated in at least eight states, including Texas, Maryland, Virginia, and Tennessee. They assisted directly with recovery efforts or stayed in their states to fill the roles of the state National Guard units that were deployed to assist in the recovery. SDFs have also offered critical infrastructure protection. In Operation Noble Eagle, the homeland defense and civil support operation after

9/11, the Alaskan SDF aided in the efforts to protect the Alaska oil pipeline.

History suggests that State Defense Forces may be most valuable in assisting the states in emergency response. In the event of a natural or man-made disaster, the first tier of response is state and local first responders. However, Hurricane Katrina exposed a vital difference between a "normal" disaster and a catastrophic disaster. A catastrophic disaster quickly stresses the resources and capabilities of state and local responders. In such cases, the Title 32 National Guard troops can serve as the second tier of response. Yet given the National Guard's high operational tempo over the past decade, the state Guard units may be unavailable. Likewise, the third tier, federal support in the form of reserve troops or FEMA [Federal Emergency Management Agency] assistance, may take up to 72 hours to mobilize and arrive at the scene of the disaster. In contrast, State Defense Forces are by their nature located nearby. They also know the area and the resources at hand, giving them the potential to be a key element of emergency response for the states.

Besides being readily available and continually stationed within states, SDFs can carry out state homeland security missions without any major reorganization, which would be required if Congress were to implement the Hart-Rudman Commission's recommendation to task the National Guard with this role. Furthermore, by assuming greater homeland security responsibility, SDFs would allow the National Guard to focus more on their Title 10 mission [as part of the armed forces] in the global war on terrorism. Moreover, unlike the dual-apportioned National Guard, State Defense Forces could focus more completely on homeland security than the National Guard.

Underfunded and Undersupported

State Defense Forces offer an important homeland security asset to many states, but several challenges have prevented these forces from reaching their full potential. Existing SDFs are often underfunded and undersupported, and some vulnerable states have not yet formed SDFs.

One of the greatest challenges to the creation and maintenance of State Defense Forces across the nation is ignorance among state and national security leaders. Many of these leaders are fundamentally unaware of the existence and capabilities of SDFs. This is largely a public relations nightmare for the SDFs because this general ignorance greatly impedes SDF leaders' efforts to make their cause and merits known.

However, lack of awareness is not the SDFs' only major public relations challenge. Often those who are aware of SDFs confuse them with private militia forces associated with radical organizations. State Defense Forces are the modern state militias. These forces are government-authorized, organized, professional militias, in sharp contrast to their radical "counterparts."

SDFs are also limited by the restriction forbidding them from receiving in-kind support from the U.S. Department of Defense (DOD). While SDFs should remain funded solely by the states, in-kind support in the form of equipment and facilities would enhance SDF training and capabilities. However, because the DOD does not directly support SDFs, they cannot use federal resources, even surplus federal equipment and supplies. This is particularly challenging given that many SDFs work closely with their state National Guards. Nevertheless, SDFs are not permitted to use Guard facilities, trucks, or equipment, even when state National Guard troops are deployed elsewhere and SDFs are filling in during their absence. . . .

There are clear historical, legal, and practical justifications for strengthening the State Defense Forces. Since the founding of this country, militias have played a vital role in fulfilling the constitutional duty of providing for the common defense. Today, as strictly state forces, SDFs continue to provide critical manpower at minimal cost.

Despite the undeniable benefits from having an effective SDF, many SDFs lack the resources and the operational standards needed to make them more effective. Some states at high risk of natural or man-made disasters have not even formed SDFs. The U.S. and its states can no longer afford to sideline these national security assets.

*"State defense forces became a haven
for right-wing extremists, 'Rambo
wannabes' and white supremacists."*

State Defense Forces Are Unnecessary and Can Be Dangerous

Judy L. Thomas

Judy L. Thomas is a projects reporter for the Kansas City (MO)
Star. *In the following viewpoint she reports that the Missouri
Militia hopes to become a state defense force. She notes, however,
that many state officials resist creating a state defense force. This
is because, she says, such forces are not seen as necessary for disaster response. In addition, she reports, many experts and state
officials worry that a state defense force may harbor extremists or
neo-Nazis.*

As you read, consider the following questions:

1. According to Thomas, why did lawmakers order an investigation of the Virginia Defense Force in 1990?
2. Who is J.T. Ready and what group is he trying to reactivate, according to the author?

3. Who is Glenn Reynolds and what is his view of state militias, as given by Thomas?

Members of the Missouri Militia envision a day when they will be called upon to assist state and local authorities—even the National Guard—in times of emergency.

The militia hopes for legislation that would officially recognize it as a volunteer "state guard" or "state defense force," ready to respond to natural disasters and civil unrest.

"We would welcome the chance to be of use to the state," said Randy Sumpter, a colonel of the Missouri Militia's 1st Battalion/3rd Brigade.

That may seem to be an unusual ambition, but such state auxiliary forces already exist.

In fact, Texas has a state guard that Gov. Rick Perry activated in June [2010] to assist with the response to Hurricane Alex. More than 750 members were called to duty to open and maintain shelters and assist the American Red Cross.

But critics contend that state defense forces can attract extreme elements.

In 1990, for example, lawmakers ordered an investigation of the Virginia Defense Force after receiving complaints that members were saving up money to buy a tank. Utah's governor dismantled the Utah State Guard in 1987 after authorities discovered that some officers in the guard had practiced assassinations.

It may be an uphill battle to establish new forces.

An attempt to create one in Oklahoma earlier this year [2010] hit a brick wall in the Legislature, and a similar measure in Montana died last year in a House committee.

Missouri officials aren't enthusiastic about the idea, either.

"We've got about 11,000 members of the Missouri National Guard and the Army National Guard and the Air National Guard," said Scott Holste, a spokesman for Gov. Jay Nixon. "The

Guard really has shown itself to be capable of responding not only to the natural disasters we've had in Missouri, but also in carrying out its mission when those units have been deployed to the Middle East."

State guards are hardly a new concept, yet few people are aware they even exist. Indeed, 22 states—but not Missouri or Kansas—have active state defense forces. Besides the Texas State Guard that helped after Hurricane Alex [South Texas, 2010], the California State Military Reserve helps that state's National Guard troops with security at the Los Alamitos Joint Forces Training Base.

A de facto force already is operating in Arizona.

J.T. Ready, a neo-Nazi who recently began conducting heavily armed desert patrols in search of "narco-terrorists" and illegal immigrants in Pinal County, told *The Kansas City Star* that he was working on a proposal seeking state approval for his group, the U.S. Border Guard.

"I'm putting together a package and presenting it to the Arizona Legislature and saying, 'Why don't we go ahead and make the border rangers official, or completely reactivate the Arizona Rangers and we'll work together,'" he said.

The Arizona Rangers were created in 1901 to protect the territory from outlaws and rustlers. The group was re-established in 1957.

But watchdog groups say Ready's patrol illustrates why states should not sanction defense forces.

"We know that the neo-Nazis carry guns, but here's an example of neo-Nazis with guns trying to position themselves to become an instrument of state policy," said Leonard Zeskind, the president of the Kansas City–based Institute for Research and Education on Human Rights.

Mark Pitcavage, a historian and the director of investigative research for the Anti-Defamation League, said state defense forces became popular in World War I because of a concern that if National Guard troops were sent overseas, there wouldn't be anyone left to deal with civil unrest at home. The state defense forces diminished after World War II.

In the 1980s, there was a resurgence when the [Ronald] Reagan administration encouraged states to begin forming them again.

Many members of the groups were retired military personnel, Pitcavage said, and others were "weekend warriors" who enjoyed the notion of serving. But increasingly, the state defense forces became a haven for right-wing extremists, "Rambo wannabes" and white supremacists, Pitcavage said.

"Individuals could conduct paramilitary training, indulge in military fantasies and even claim a mantle of legality and legitimacy," he said.

Pitcavage said extremists infiltrated some units and took over others. Some states, he said, had to purge units and even ban their entire forces because of it.

In Virginia, the General Assembly launched an investigation of its state defense force in 1990 after hearing that a brigade was saving up to purchase a tank and some units were practicing drug raids. A few years earlier, authorities discovered that some Utah State Guardsmen were neo-Nazis and felons, and some officers had practiced assassinations and conducted commando desert exercises with live ammunition.

In 1984, a Vietnam War veteran who led a Texas State Guard unit was ousted for engaging his group in Rambo-style paramilitary training that included parachute jumps.

"To this day, a lot of people involved in those groups are completely flaky," Pitcavage said.

But Glenn Reynolds, a law professor at the University of Tennessee and an expert on militias, said he saw no problem with such groups being involved with state defense forces.

"It's not some crazy idea that someone has come up with out of the blue," Reynolds said. "Historically, that's how militias were organized. It's sort of back to the future." Reynolds, the author of the widely read political blog Instapundit, said the state defense force has operated in Tennessee for many years.

"I've never heard any problems about it," he said.

Periodical and Internet Sources Bibliography

The following articles have been selected to supplement the diverse views presented in this chapter.

Ray Hartwell	"Hartwell: Obama Lawsuit Invites Fortified State Militia," *Washington Times*, July 16, 2010. www .washingtontimes.com.
Ted Lang	"The National Guard Is Not the Militia—Armed Citizens Are!," Rense.com, May 25, 2005.
Robert A. Levy	"*District of Columbia v. Heller*: What's Next?," Cato Unbound, July 14, 2008. www.cato-unbound.org.
Nelson Lund	"Second Amendment, *Heller*, and Originalist Jurisprudence," Social Science Research Network, May 1, 2009. http://papers.ssrn.com.
National Guard	"About the National Guard," n.d., www.ng.mil.
John F. Romano	"State Militias and the United States: Changed Responsibilities for a New Era," *Air Force Law Review*, Winter 2005. http:// findarticles.com.
Straight Dope	"What's the National Guard Doing Fighting Overseas, Anyway?," July 21, 2009. www.straightdope .com.
Juli Weiner	"The Oklahoma Legislature and the Tea Party Want YOU to Join Their Volunteer Militia Army!," *Vanity Fair*, April 13, 2010. www .vanityfair.com.
Jessica Zuckerman	"The Not So Secret World of State Militias," *The Foundry* (blog), October 12, 2010. http://blog .heritage.org.

**OPPOSING
VIEWPOINTS®
SERIES**

What Is the Relationship Between Christianity and Militias?

Chapter Preface

Christian Identity is a racist, Eurocentric interpretation of Christianity, which holds that white Europeans, not Jews, are the true descendents of the biblical Israelites. Dennis Tourish and Tim Wohlforth in a 2001 article argue that "many white supremacist organizations in the United States (such as Posse Comitatus, Aryan Nations and innumerable militia groups) draw their inspiration from a theology known as Christian Identity." The Jewish Anti-Defamation League (ADL) also links Christian Identity with the militia movement in a 2005 article on its website. "The influence of Identity often extends beyond Identity circles," the ADL notes. "The Militia of Montana, which helped create the militia movement, is headed by Identity adherents, though they do not promote the theology," the ADL further asserts.

Though Christian Identity groups see themselves as Christians, they actually have a very hostile relationship with conservative fundamentalist churches. This is because "the Christian Identity movement is a significant departure from the doctrines of mainstream Christianity, most notably in its racism," according to James J.F. Forest in volume 3 of the 2007 book *Countering Terrorism and Insurgency in the 21st Century*. Forest notes that while fundamentalist Christians make no effort to theologically justify racism, Christian Identity groups argue that anti-Semitism and racism are biblically based. Forest writes that Christian Identity also espouses an apocalyptic ideology; it believes that "the world is on the brink of a great apocalyptic confrontation between the Aryans and the Jews. . . . "

This mixture of racism and apocalyptic rhetoric led a number of Christian Identity adherents to commit violent acts, especially in the 1990s. In a March 5, 2000, *St. Louis Post-Dispatch* article, Carolyn Tuft and Joe Holleman reported that since 1990, "Identity followers have been tied to murder, robbery and kidnapping." Tuft and Holleman pointed, for example, to Buford O.

Furrow, who in August 2000 "killed a postal worker and wounded five others after opening fire on a Jewish day-care center in Los Angeles." Tuft and Holleman also argue that the Identity movement was linked through militias to the Oklahoma City bombing in 1995.

The Southern Poverty Law Center in its discussion of Christian Identity notes that "a prolonged period of aggressive efforts by law enforcement" and the deaths of key leaders has significantly reduced the influence of Christian Identity in the 2000s. Thus, for example, the Oklahoma Constitutional Militia, a small group that planned to bomb "gay bars, abortion clinics, and civil rights groups," was broken up by the FBI and its members put in prison in the mid-1990s, according to the organization's profile on the website of START, the National Consortium for the Study of Terrorism and Responses to Terrorism. Nonetheless, the Christian Identity movement has not vanished altogether and continues to be an influence on white supremacist groups like Aryan Nations.

The viewpoints in the following chapter debate other ways in which the militia movement is, or is not, linked to Christian religious beliefs.

> "The view that gun ownership is a
> Christian duty, rooted in the overlap
> between Reconstructionism and the
> survivalist/militia movement, has
> become common in both."

The Militia Movement Is Linked to Christian Extremism

Sarah Posner and Julie Ingersoll

Sarah Posner is the associate editor of the e-zine and blog Religion Dispatches *and the author of* God's Profits: Faith, Fraud, and the Republican Crusade for Values Voters. *Julie Ingersoll is a professor of religion at the University of North Florida. In the following viewpoint, they report on Christian Reconstructionism, a radical Christian ideology. Christian Reconstructionism, they assert, contends that the Bible calls for Christians to defend themselves from tyranny. Christian Reconstructionists support gun rights as part of a radical agenda to promote religious law and resist the tyrannical power of the federal government, the authors maintain. They link Christian Reconstructionism to both the Tea Party and the militia movement.*

As you read, consider the following questions:

1. Why was Judge Ray Moore stripped of his position, according to the authors?

2. According to Posner and Ingersoll, among what institutions does Herb Titus believe that authority is distributed by God?

3. How do the authors define the Tenth Amendment Movement?

Herb Titus, a lawyer for the far-right Gun Owners of America [GOA], is jubilant over last week's [early July 2010] Supreme Court decision in the case *McDonald v. City of Chicago*, finding that state and local regulation of gun ownership must comport with the Second Amendment right to bear arms.

Guns and Christian Reconstructionism

The decision has also pleased the National Rifle Association, which sees it as ammunition for challenging gun control laws across the country. But for Titus, who thinks the NRA "compromises" on gun rights, the Second Amendment isn't solely about "firepower," he says. "You have to see it in its spiritual and providential perspective."

That perspective is about far more than hunting and self-defense. For Titus, the Court's 2008 recognition of an individual right to bear arms, and its application of that principle to the states in the *McDonald* case, are crucial steps toward arming Americans against their own government. Titus cites the "totalitarian threat" posed by "Obamacare" [the health care reform passed under President Barack Obama in 2010] and "what [2008 Republican vice presidential candidate] Sarah Palin said about death panels." [Palin claimed that health care reform would mean the bureaucrats would deny care to the elderly or terminally ill.] People need to be armed, he said, "because ultimately it may come to the point where it's a life and death situation."

Titus, who filed an *amicus* brief on behalf of the GOA, an organization which claims 300,000 members, told RD [*Religion Dispatches*] that "the ultimate authority is God."

"[I]f you have a people that has basically been disarmed by the civil government," he added, "then there really isn't any effectual means available to the people to restore law and liberty and that's really the purpose of the right keep and bear arms—is to defend yourself against a tyrant."

If this sounds like standard-issue Tea Party fodder, it's because the Tea Party movement emerges out of the confluence of different strands of the far right, including Christian Reconstructionism. Titus has long been a player at the intersection of Christian Reconstructionism, the standard religious right, and other far-right groups in which the Tea Party finds its roots. He was a speaker at the Reconstructionist American Vision's annual "Worldview Conference" in 2009, has been a member of the Council for National Policy, and is a longtime homeschooling advocate from a Reconstructionist perspective. In 1996 he was the running mate of conservative icon (and Christian Reconstructionist) Howard Phillips for the far-right US Taxpayers Party (now called the Constitution Party) whose platform included the restoration of "American jurisprudence to its biblical premises" and, notably, opposition to every gun law in the United States.

Now a lawyer with the firm William J. Olson, P.C., Titus was a founding dean of Pat Robertson's Regent University Law School, where he was the chair of a three-member committee that supervised Virginia Governor Bob McDonnell's now-notorious graduate thesis. In it, a recitation of the religious right's agenda, McDonnell called working women and feminists "detrimental" to the family, argued for policy favoring married couples over "cohabitators, homosexuals, or fornicators," and called the 1972 legalization of contraception by married couples "illogical."

During his 2009 campaign, McDonnell tried to distance himself from his own work, but Titus told the *Washington Post* that McDonnell's thesis was "right."

In 2004, after Judge Roy Moore, another Titus client, was stripped of his position for defying a federal court order to remove his 2.6-ton monument to the Ten Commandments from the rotunda of the Alabama Supreme Court, he joined Titus in drafting the Constitution Restoration Act. The bill, had it passed, would have deprived federal courts of jurisdiction to hear cases challenging a government entity's or official's "acknowledgment of God as the sovereign source of law, liberty, or government."

This clear articulation of the religious right's dominionist aims, framed as a challenge to what the Right asserts is the excessive power of the federal government, did manage to receive Republican support. It had nine co-sponsors in the Senate and was introduced in the House by Alabama Republican Robert Aderholt, who had 50 co-sponsors, including now-Minority Whip Eric Cantor, now-Louisiana Governor Bobby Jindal, and Rep. Mike Pence, who is thought to be considering a 2012 presidential run.

Militias, the Religious Right, and Biblical Law

The militia movement and Christian Reconstructionism both contend that our current civil government, most especially the federal government, is illegitimate: that it has overreached the limits of its divinely ordained authority, and that it continues to do so. At this intersection of the religious right and the militia movement, gun ownership is portrayed as a religious issue. "When we're talking about firearms," GOA executive director Larry Pratt told RD, "we're not really talking about a right but an obligation, as creatures of God, to protect the life that was given them."

Many in the militia movement, the Tea Party Movement, and Christian Reconstruction also share the view that civil government should be reformed according to the dictates of biblical law.

In describing the "fundamental issue" as "God's authority," Titus echoes themes from Christian Reconstructionist founder R.J. Rushdoony, including the notion that civil government has certain limits established by God. Although Titus, who earned his law degree from Harvard in 1962, claims he is not a Reconstructionist, he doesn't deny its influence on his thinking, acknowledging how, after he was saved in 1975, his new jurisprudence was shaped by Rushdoony's seminal text, *The Institutes of Biblical Law.*

Like Rushdoony, Titus argues that government is by covenant; that authority is distributed by God among three institutions with distinct (and distinctly limited) jurisdictions: family, church, and civil government. To root this view in the American Constitutional system, Rushdoony and Titus both read the secular language of the Constitution in the context of the invocation of "the Creator" in the Declaration of Independence: "Inalienable rights are endowed by the Creator." These rights, both Rushdoony and Titus contend, are not granted by either document, only recognized in them; these rights exist only because they were granted by God.

Because Supreme Court nominee Elena Kagan refused to acknowledge the divine source of the Constitution, and in particular the Second Amendment, Titus believes she is not qualified to serve on the Court. (Titus' law partner testified on behalf of the GOA against Kagan's confirmation, one of several witnesses called by the Republicans.) Echoing the Christian Reconstructionist view, Sen. Charles Grassley asked Kagan, "did the Second Amendment codify a preexisting right or was it a right created by the Constitution?"—something Kagan, not surprisingly, said she'd never contemplated.

"Here's a woman who's being nominated to sit on the United States Supreme Court and she's never thought about the question [of] whether rights are given by God or given by men," Titus exclaimed incredulously. "She's never even considered it!"

The Christian Duty to Take Up Arms

While many gun advocates are concerned with preserving access to firearms for hunting, and others argue that the right to possession of firearms is essential for self-defense against criminals, Reconstructionists have a loftier argument: so Christians can exercise their duty to take up arms against a government that has exceeded its bounds established by God.

In this view, when the civil government oversteps the authority given to it by God, citizens have a right and an obligation to resist. Titus insists it is "the basis upon which this nation was founded. We were a well-armed people, and when the call came to come out and to fight the redcoats, people were armed— pastors, and their parishioners. They came out and defended their liberties."

The view that gun ownership is a Christian duty, rooted in the overlap between Reconstructionism and the survivalist/ militia movement, has become common in both. In his "Bring Your Pieces to Church" Sunday essay, Reconstructionist Joel McDurmon makes this point, suggesting that believers should organize target practice after church:

> Christians should be aware that the use of force in preservation of life is a biblical doctrine. Likewise, those who possessed weapons in Scripture are often said to be well skilled in the use of them. We can only surmise that 1) God gave them talent in this regard, and that 2) they engaged in target practice regularly. Further, under biblical law, to be disarmed was to be enslaved and led to a disruption of the economic order due to government regulations and monopolies.

Reconstructionists are critical of those who defend the Second Amendment only in terms of hunting. They believe that

The Influence of Christian Reconstruction

Reconstruction is the spark plug behind much of the battle over religion in politics today. The movement's founder, theologian Rousas John Rushdoony, claimed 20 million followers—a number that includes many who embrace the Reconstruction tenets without having joined any organization. Card-carrying Reconstructionists are few, but their influence is magnified by their leadership in Christian right crusades, from abortion to homeschooling.

Reconstructionists also exert significant clout through front organizations and coalitions with other religious fundamentalists; Baptists, Anglicans, and others have deep theological differences with the movement, but they have made common cause with its leaders in groups such as the National Coalition for Revival. Reconstruction has slowly absorbed, congregation by congregation, the conservative Presbyterian Church in America . . . and has heavily influenced others, notably the Southern Baptists.

John Sugg, Mother Jones, *December 2005.*

the protection of a sporting activity would not have been the basis of an amendment to the Constitution intended to protect basic rights that were fundamental to liberty. McDurmon also points to widespread gun ownership as a defense against tyranny, tracing the colonial laws that required gun ownership and arguing that "in the context of the War for Independence, ministers saw guns as tools of liberty and defense against tyranny." In fact, he argues that gun ownership by individuals should be the basis of national defense and that a standing army is unbiblical.

. . . And the Tea Party

Rep. Ron Paul, a godfather of sorts to the Tea Parties, calls the GOA "the only no-compromise gun lobby in Washington." Indeed, Pratt, GOA's executive director, told RD that he has spoken at Tea Party events, calling his group "a natural match for the folks in the Tea Party." Pratt believes the federal government is largely unconstitutional, and that all federal agencies save the Department of Justice and the Department of the Treasury (which should be "a lot smaller"), should be abolished. (The Internal Revenue Service is a part of Treasury that Pratt would like to see abolished.)

GOA's political action arm has endorsed Paul's son, Rand, in the Kentucky Senate race, as well as other Tea Party favorites for Senate: Sharron Angle (Nevada), Marco Rubio (Florida), J.D. Hayworth (Arizona), David Vitter (Louisiana), Tom Coburn (Oklahoma), and Jim DeMint (South Carolina), as well as eight House candidates. The Angle campaign embraced the endorsement, with her spokesperson saying, "Not only is Mrs. Angle unafraid of guns, but she is also unafraid to stand up against those who would attempt to deny the legal rights of other gun owners."

Pratt, whose advocacy has led him to intersect not only with the Tea Partiers, but also with neo-Nazis and white supremacists, sees the revitalization of the 10th Amendment movement— far-right agitators who believe the federal government is largely unconstitutional—as evidence of states "pushing back federal authority." Pratt believes that states should be "reactivating" militias; which should be at their disposal "instead of relying on the [federal] government to come and screw things up . . . these things should be given new life."

Pratt refuses the label "Christian Reconstructionist," telling RD he prefers to identify as a "Biblical Christian." He advocates for militias which he describes as "the sheriff's posse" and that the "availability of it will further cool their [the federal government's] jets. No more Wacos [in 1993, federal agents set siege to

179

the compound of a radical-right group in Waco, Texas, eventually resulting in the deaths of more than seventy people]. Because if you try something like that again, we're not going to stand around and watch. We're going to put you in our jail. Which is what the sheriff in that county should have told the thugs in Waco."

This is predicated, Pratt insists, "on the actual meaning of the word *militia*, as it was put into the Constitution and into the Bill of Rights."

Citing Romans 13 [in the Bible's New Testament], Pratt said the "magistrate is a servant of God. He's supposed to be a terror to evildoers and a comfort to the righteous. So we talk in terms of protecting the people's liberties. That's really the same concept."

In an essay posted on the GOA Web site, "What Does The Bible Say About Gun Control?," Pratt argues that "resisting an attack is not to be confused with taking vengeance, which is the exclusive domain of God," citing Romans 12:19. That domain of God, he maintains, "has been delegated to the civil magistrate" who is "God's minister, an avenger to execute wrath on him who practices evil."

Likewise, Titus, in his interview with RD, referred to this notion of legitimate civil uprising or resistance resting on the support of "lesser magistrates." This concept derives from [sixteenth-century religious reformer John] Calvin but is a concept central to Reconstructionism—that Christians are obligated to obey civil authority because it is delegated by God; they can only resist one civil authority when in submission to another one. Put in secular terms, this dovetails with their longstanding support for "states' rights" and their desire to see organized militias that can be called up by state governors (who are "lesser magistrates") for the defense of a state against what they claim is the tyrannical overreach of the federal government.

With the receptivity of the Tea Party Movement to arguments against supposed excessive federal power, Christian Reconstructionist–inspired militias could find new converts.

Pratt said that when he speaks about his militia idea at Tea Party rallies, "it's very well-received." It may be "a new idea in the details," he added, "but it certainly resonates instantly with them."

> *"The [arrested militia members] are not 'Christian jihadists.' Their alleged plans are not based on Christian doctrine."*

Extremist Militias Do Not Represent Christianity

Artemis Gordon Glidden

Artemis Gordon Glidden is a software engineer and musician living in the San Francisco Bay Area in California; he blogs at The Iconoclast *on the site of the* New English Review. *In the following viewpoint, Glidden argues that there is no biblical basis for violence against the government. On the other hand, he contends, there is such a basis in Islamic teaching. Therefore, he maintains, it makes sense to think of Islamic terrorists as Islamic, but violent militias like the Hutaree cannot be considered Christian. He adds that the Hutaree, in planning violence against police, are not patriotic, but in fact hate the American system of government.*

As you read, consider the following questions:

1. What does John 15:13 say, and where did Glidden find this biblical passage quoted?
2. According to the author, who calls for violent jihad against non-Muslims?

3. What does Glidden say the fight agaist jihad mostly consists of?

This AP [Associated Press] story about the Christian militia group arrested today [March 30, 2010] contains this quote:

> Hutaree says on its Web site its name means "Christian warrior" and describes the word as part of a secret language few are privileged to know. The group quotes several Bible passages. . . .

Biblical Quotations

I was curious about what kind of Biblical quotations a Christian militia would use on their website. Their website contains these quotations:

John 15:13: "Greater love hath no man than this, that a man lay down his life for his friends."

Hebrews 11:1: "Faith is the substance of things hoped for, The Evidence of things not yet seen."

I Peter 5:11: "And this is the Testimony, that God has given us eternal life, and this life is in his Son."

Revelation 3:19: "Jesus told the Church of Laodicea, 'As many as I love, I rebuke and chasten: be zealous therefore, and repent.'"

Jeremiah 4:1–4: "If thou wilt return, O Israel, saith the LORD, return unto me: and if thou wilt put away thine abominations out of my sight, then shalt thou not remove. And thou shalt swear, The LORD liveth, in truth, in judgment, and in righteousness; and the nations shall bless themselves in him, and in him shall they glory. For thus saith the LORD to the men of Judah and Jerusalem, Break up your fallow ground, and sow not among thorns. Circumcise yourselves to the LORD, and take away the foreskins of your heart, ye men of Judah and inhabitants of Jerusalem: lest my fury come forth like fire, and burn that none can quench it, because of the evil of your doings."

Jeremiah 24:7: "And I will give them an heart to know me, that I am the LORD: and they shall be my people, and I will be their God: for they shall return unto me with their whole heart."

Luke 13:1–5: "There were present at that season some that told him of the Galilaeans, whose blood Pilate had mingled with their sacrifices. And Jesus answering said unto them, Suppose ye that these Galilaeans were sinners above all the Galilaeans, because they suffered such things? I tell you, Nay: but, except ye repent, ye shall all likewise perish. Or those eighteen, upon whom the tower in Siloam fell, and slew them, think ye that they were sinners above all men that dwelt in Jerusalem? I tell you, Nay: but, except ye repent, ye shall all likewise perish."

Genesis 3:7–10: "And the eyes of them both were opened, and they knew that they were naked; and they sewed fig leaves together, and made themselves aprons. And they heard the voice of the LORD God walking in the garden in the cool of the day: and Adam and his wife hid themselves from the presence of the LORD God amongst the trees of the garden. And the LORD God called unto Adam, and said unto him, Where art thou? And he said, I heard thy voice in the garden, and I was afraid, because I was naked; and I hid myself."

Genesis 3:12: "And the man said, The woman whom thou gavest to be with me, she gave me of the tree, and I did eat."

Genesis 3:13: "And the woman said, The serpent beguiled me, and I did eat."

2 Corinthians 7:10: "For godly sorrow worketh repentance to salvation not to be repented of: but the sorrow of the world worketh death.

Acts 2:37: "Now when they heard this, they were pricked in their heart, and said unto Peter and to the rest of the apostles, Men and brethren, what shall we do?"

Matthew 27:3–5: "Then Judas, which had betrayed him, when he saw that he was condemned, repented himself, and brought again the thirty pieces of silver to the chief priests and elders, saying, I have sinned in that I have betrayed the innocent blood.

And they said, What is that to us? see thou to that. And he cast down the pieces of silver in the temple, and departed, and went and hanged himself."

Not Motivated by the Bible

Nothing shocking there. Nothing about killing policemen. Nothing about killing, period. If the members of Hutaree are actually guilty of planning attacks on police, government officials, and Muslims, their plans were not based on following the words of the Bible. There are no "Slay the non-believers wherever you find them" verses [as in the Qur'an] on their website, or in the Bible. Whatever motivated them, it was not Biblical quotations.

Compare and contrast that to the Qur'anic quotations of jihadists that unambiguously call for faithful Muslims to commit violence against non-Muslims. The quote from AP was intended, I believe, to suggest an equivalence between the Hutaree group and Muslim jihadists, when in fact there is no equivalence at all. There are no mainstream Christian scholars who teach that the Bible calls for the murder of policemen, government officials, or Muslims. However, there *are* mainstream Islamic scholars, the most respected senior Islamic scholars in the most devoutly Islamic nations, that *do* teach that the Qur'an calls for violent jihad against non-Muslims. They provide the quotations, and anyone can look them up and verify their authenticity and their relevance.

Here are some other quotes from the AP story:

Prosecutors said David Stone had identified certain law enforcement officers near his home as potential targets. He and other members discussed setting off bombs at a police funeral, using a fake 911 call to lure an officer to his death, killing an officer after a traffic stop, or attacking the family of an officer, according to the indictment. . . .

And:

[Kelly Sickles, wife of one of the arrested men] said she couldn't believe her 27-year-old husband could be involved in anything violent. "It was just survival skills," she said. "That's what they were learning. And it's just patriotism. It's in our Constitution."

The Opposite of Patriotism

Now, please. There is nothing patriotic about trying to start an uprising against the government. We have a democratic republic, which has mechanisms for concerned citizens to get involved and influence public policy. That does not include using explosives or attacking the family of a police officer. If the Hutaree think that our government is so corrupt that the only solution is to start blowing people up, they are the exact opposites of patriots. They hate our system of government, they hate the members of our society.

If the Hutaree planned to kill Muslims in our country, they are dangerous and belong in prison. The fight against jihad does not justify individuals to take the law into their own hands and become judge, jury, and executioners. This is not Pakistan, or Saudi Arabia, or the Sudan. Our government does not kill people because of their religious affiliation, nor does it sanction citizens to do so. The fight against jihad is mostly educational, in teaching non-Muslims about what Islam actually teaches. The fight against jihad is defensive, it is about protecting our rights and protecting our physical safety.

Regardless of how they are portrayed in the media, the Hutarees are not "Christian jihadists." Their alleged plans are not based on Christian doctrine.

> *"It's time to get real—the Bible is a dangerous book for mentally unstable people."*

Extremist Christian Militias Demonstrate the Dangers of Religious Belief

CJ Werleman

CJ Werleman is the author of God Hates You, Hate Him Back: Making Sense of the Bible. *In the following viewpoint he discusses the right-wing violent Christian militia group known as the Hutaree. He argues that the Hutaree views are no more dangerous or ridiculous than those of any of the major religions. He notes that the Bible's Old and New Testaments both encourage violence. He concludes that the Bible is a dangerous book liable to be used as a justification for horrible acts by the mentally unstable and those with poor reasoning skills.*

As you read, consider the following questions:

1. With what were the Hutaree charged, according to Werleman?
2. According to the author, what does the commandment

"thou shalt not kill" mean in the Hebrew Bible?

3. What does Werleman suggest in order to prevent people from harming themselves by reading the Bible?

Nine members of a rightwing Christian militia in Michigan were arrested yesterday [March 30, 2010], charged with plotting to murder a policeman and then bomb his funeral. Their overarching objective being to provoke an anti-government uprising.

Self-Deluded Crackpots

The group call themselves the Hutaree militia, but you can think of them as just another regiment of self-deluded crackpots that believe the government has hatched a plot to take away their Bibles and guns. No doubt, you are probably asking yourself what does 'Hutaree' mean? Well, according to their website it means "Christian warrior" and proclaims on its home page:

"Preparing for the end time battles to keep the testimony of Jesus Christ alive."

A click on the "About Us" tab of the group's website, reveals the following statement:

"We believe that one day, as prophecy says, there will be an Anti-Christ. All Christians must know this and prepare, just as Christ commanded."

Ok, here's my point: by what standard do we call these nine Christians, crazy? Are they insane for believing a prophecy from an ancient text (the Bible) to be relevant in the first place, or are they just plain crazy for wanting to kill innocent folk?

I would contend that all believers of the three monotheistic faiths are philosophically prohibited to label the Hutaree militia as anything other than a religious group of dogmatic faith. Jesus

© Bruce Plante-Tulsa World.

and Yahweh want you—nah, scratch that—demand of you to kill anyone that stands in the way of worshipping them.

Jesus prophesized the Biblical end times to look like this:

> Brother shall deliver up his brother to death, and the father the child: and the children shall rise up against their parents, and cause them to be put to death.

Yahweh hops aboard the 'straight-talk express', when he says to Moses:

> If your very own brother, or your son or daughter, or the wife you love, or your closest friend secretly entices you, saying, 'Let's go out and worship other gods', do not yield to him or listen to him. Show him no pity. Do not spare him or shield him. You must certainly put him to death. Your hand must be the first in putting him to death and then the hands of the people.

The Bible Is Dangerous

Killing and blowing up shit is all part of the Christian deal. It was Jesus that said, "I have not come to bring peace but a sword." If Jesus were alive today—a modernized version of his proclamation would read "I have not come to bring peace but a dirty great big f---ing bomb." And let's not forget that Jesus gave his full and unwavering endorsement to all 613 commandments of the Old Testament, including the infanticide, slavery, and genocide decrees. Now, before you point to the 'thou shall not kill' clause—understand that in context of the ancient Hebrew meaning, this law meant 'thou shall not kill Hebrews.'

Therefore, is it not their religious text that made these nine crazy, and by reverse logic—are not these religious books dangerous to public health?

It's time to get real—the Bible is a dangerous book for mentally unstable people; people who have a tendency to believe unsubstantiated promises; or those lacking critical thinking skills. Our movies, food, drink, and medicine come packaged with the proper warning labels—so as to prevent doing harm to ourselves. Isn't it fair to apply the same standard to books from antiquity, whose authors believed murdering your child for working on a holy day to be a morally justifiable action?

If my monthly subscription of *Playboy* magazine comes blazoned with a warning label across its cover, then why not the same treatment for the Bible and the Koran? An appropriate warning for these respective holy books could look something like this:

CONTENT ADVISORY:
Contains verses descriptive [of] or advocating suicide, incest, bestiality, sadomasochism, sexual activity in a violent context, murder, morbid violence, voyeurism, revenge, undermining of authority figures, lawlessness and human rights violations and atrocities.

EXPOSURE WARNING:

Exposure to contents for extended periods of time or during formative years in children may cause delusions, hallucinations, decrease cognitive and objective reasoning abilities, and in extreme cases, pathological disorders, hatred, bigotry, violence including but not limited to fanaticism, murder and genocide.

*"It seems that we have seen the first use
of a new government tactic: The use
of Muslim militias . . . to entrap and
destroy Christian communities."*

Attacks on Militias Show
Anti-Christian Bias

James Sanchez

James Sanchez has written for the American Mercury *and the*
Media Monitors Network. *In the following viewpoint, he argues
that members of the Hutaree militia group are not dangerous and
that they have been framed by law enforcement. He points out that
the Hutaree surrendered peacefully when arrested and argues that
the most inflammatory material on their website may have been
planted by the FBI. He suggests that the government has allied itself with Muslim groups and has undertaken a systematic campaign against Christian communities.*

As you read, consider the following questions:

1. According to Sanchez, what group lauded the FBI for its
   arrest of the Hutaree?
2. What groups does the author say love to hear about the
   Hutaree plot?

3. What does Sanchez predict will happen to the members of the Hutaree?

I had never heard of the [militia group the] Hutaree. Seemingly, the Hutaree were a vast conspiracy that wanted to kill police officers as part of a plot to start a race war or something. The FBI supposedly became aware of it when a member of a national news organization passed a tip to [the] Council on American-Islamic Relations, which in turn contacted the FBI.

FBI Actions Against the Hutaree

Then raids were staged in several states. Everywhere the Hutaree surrendered peacefully and without incident. One group tried to escape and ran to their contact in the Southeast Michigan Volunteer Militia, a Muslim(!), but he refused to help them. Before their Web site and computers were seized (by the FBI) and flooded with homosexual pornography: "a member of the Hutaree posted a message online pleading for help and claiming that officials 'broke into homes and took children and used the tasers on wives . . . *AND* my son who is 12'" [according to an ABC News report]. (Torturing wives and children is an old Israeli technique and it has been commonly used in the War on Terrorism: [accused terrorist] Khalid Sheikh Mohammed's 8- and 10-year old sons were captured before he was and the US boasted in Pakistan that they were being tortured. So TASERing children to extract information from their watching parents has, apparently, just become routine.)

What? One of the Michigan Militia leaders is *Muslim*? Moreover someone in close contact with the Hutaree, trusted by the Hutaree who believed him trustworthy enough to hide them from the police, and who lived very close to the Hutaree . . . Indeed, and the Muslim turns out to be an informant for the FBI: "One of the Hutaree members called a Michigan militia leader for assistance Saturday after federal agents had already began [sic] their raid, [Mike Lackomar of Michiganmilitia.com] said, but the militia member—who is of Islamic decent and had heard about the threats—declined to offer help. That Michigan militia leader is now working with federal officials to provide information on the Hutaree member for the investigation, Lackomar said" [according to the *Detroit News*].

Meanwhile, the African-American-Muslim MAS [Muslim American Society] Freedom Foundation, fresh from its [Washington,] DC conference on the rights of Black cop-killers, lauds the FBI for its arrests of the Hutaree and applauds the important [if imaginary] role of the SPLC [Southern Poverty Law Center] in fighting the Christian terrorism of the Hutaree.

Canned Terrorism

I had never heard of the Hutaree. I went to their rather sad little Web site and found little of interest. Their three-document Web pages were very primitive: Hutaree. (1) About Us. N.D., (2) Doctrine of the Hutaree. N.D., and (3) Hutaree Rank System. N.D. The Hutaree documents were not extreme. They were banal and did not advocate attacks on the police. After the mass arrests by the FBI, the Web site would soon be flooded with homosexual pornography: The simplest explanation is that the homosexual pornography was posted by the FBI, emulating a trick they learned when they were trained in Israel.

Every day the Hutaree plot is refined to be marketed for broader audiences. The Oligarchic media, the left, and the Muslims love it. But it is just another canned terrorist incident, like the mildly retarded Black members of the Seas of David in Florida [arrested in 2006] or the Black dopers of the Synagogue Bombers plot in New York [in May 2009, convicted in 2010], targeting a group of social and political isolates with fantastic, heinous charges that will preclude anyone from seeing them as political victims of a government conspiracy. . . .

But there is a new element that is worth noting. In this plot against a dimwitted Christian militia, the FBI used Muslims to target Christians: Muslims to infiltrate the Hutaree (the

Muslim militiaman from whom they sought refuge, unsucess-fully), Muslims to "sound the alarm" (the Council on American-Islamic Relations, MAS Freedom Foundation, etc.), Muslims to provide intelligence (that same Muslim militiaman cited above has become a major source for the FBI against the Hutaree), and Muslims to applaud the valuable work of the SPLC (MAS Freedom Foundation).

It is not unreasonable to wonder why the Hutaree fugitives thought they could turn to that (crypto?) Muslim militiaman: Did he, for example, provide them with supplies for making pipe bombs and provide them with a contact who wanted to buy pipe bombs? One wonders.

Targeting Christians

It seems that we have seen the first use of a new government tactic: The use of Muslim militias (the Southeast Michigan Volunteer Militia is now effectively a Muslim militia, or at least a Muslim-infiltrated militia, something the SPLC would never talk about) as auxiliaries of the FBI and SPLC to entrap and destroy Christian communities. And CBS News blandly states the violent, terrorist Christian militia's motivation is that they oppose "reform" and "health care reforms," and predicts that there will be an upsurge of militia violence when "immigration reform" is undertaken later this year, especially because there is an African-American president.

Like the Seas of David, the Synagogue Bombing Plotters, and the Branch Davidians [the group attacked by federal agents in 1995 in Waco, Texas], the Hutaree are probably guilty of nothing but stupidity, and yes, they will go to prison for life after terrorism show trials.

This is what America has become.

*"Imagine if the Hutaree were not
Christian extremists, but American
Muslims? Would there be any doubt
that they would immediately be called
terrorists?"*

The Treatment of Militias Demonstrates a Pro-Christian Bias

Hesham A. Hassaballa

*Hesham A. Hassaballa is a Chicago doctor and writer. His work
has been published on Beliefnet and by the Religion News Service.
In the following viewpoint, he argues that Americans are reluc-
tant to label violent domestic Christian groups like the Hutaree
as terrorists. On the other hand, he says, any violence committed by people who are Muslim is immediately linked to terrorism.
Hassaballa argues that in fact terrorists can be of any group or
faith. He concludes that individual acts of terror should not be used
to tar entire faiths.*

As you read, consider the following questions:

1. What term does Hassaballa say the FBI omitted in its
   description of the Hutaree?

2. Who was Hesham Mohammed Hedayet, according to the author?

3. According to Hassaballa, what proportion of Americans admit to harboring hostile feelings toward Muslims?

Last month [March 2010], Federal Bureau of Investigation authorities launched several raids against a Christian militia group known as the "Hutaree." According to the authorities, members of the group had allegedly planned to kill a police officer and then kill more officers by bombing his funeral. Although widely maligned on the Right, the report by the Department of Homeland Security [DHS] was indeed correct: namely, that the threat from right-wing extremist groups is growing. In fact, the Southern Poverty Law Center, which monitors domestic hate groups, has recently corroborated the findings of the DHS. This comes on the heels of the attack on the IRS building in Texas by Joseph Stack [who flew his plane into an IRS building in February 2010] and the shooting at the Pentagon by a lone gunman [in October 2010].

Call It Terrorism

Yet, what is astonishing about these incidents, apart from the temerity of both the attacks and the alleged Hutaree plan, is the near universal reluctance to call these individuals what they truly are: domestic terrorists. Only a handful of commentators—such as Rachel Maddow, Glenn Greenwald, among a few others—have stated what is quite obvious. The *Chicago Sun-Times* actually surprised me with their headline after the arrests: "Homegrown Terror" printed over the pictures of the 9 arrested men.

Yet, the FBI Agent in charge of the investigation in Michigan said, "This is an example of radical and extremist fringe groups which can be found throughout our society. The FBI takes such extremist groups seriously." Notice the glaring absence of the word "terrorist." Yet, what else would a plan to kill a police officer

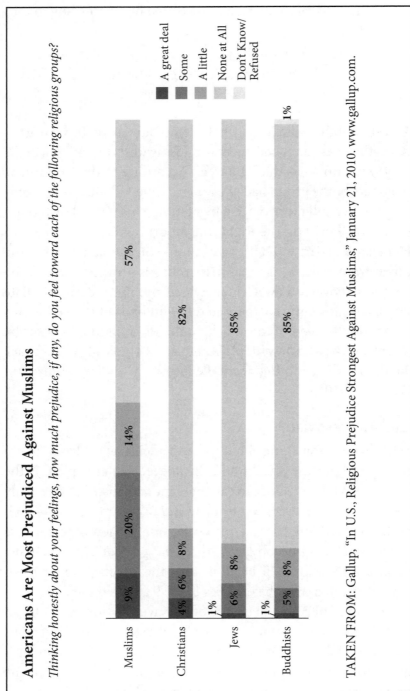

Americans Are Most Prejudiced Against Muslims

Thinking honestly about your feelings, how much prejudice, if any, do you feel toward each of the following religious groups?

- A great deal
- Some
- A little
- None at All
- Don't Know/ Refused

Muslims 9% 20% 14% 57%

Christians 4% 6% 1% 8% 82%

Jews 1% 6% 8% 85%

Buddhists 5% 8% 85% 1%

TAKEN FROM: Gallup, "In U.S., Religious Prejudice Strongest Against Muslims," January 21, 2010. www.gallup.com.

and then bomb the funeral be called except an alleged act of terrorism? Not only that, there were actually expressions of sympathy and support for the alleged Hutaree terrorists; after Joseph Stack crashed his plane into the IRS building, a Facebook page was set up in support for him, with several people calling him a "hero" (it was later taken down).

Imagine if the Hutaree were not Christian extremists, but American Muslims? Would there be any doubt that they would immediately be called terrorists? Remember Hesham Mohamed Hedayet? He was the gunman who opened fire at an El-Al [Israeli airline] counter at Los Angeles International Airport. Until the authorities confirmed that his motive was financial difficulties, everyone was screaming "terrorism." "Terror" quickly rolled off the tongues of commentators after the Fort Hood shootings, when a Muslim Army psychiatrist opened fire against his fellow soldiers. Yet, when a gunman in Florida opened fire on his co-workers almost immediately after, no one called that shooting an act of terrorism.

Islamophobia

Is there a deep-seated bias against Muslims in the minds of most Americans, which makes it easy for them to dismiss all Muslims as terrorists? Partly, perhaps. Recent polls have indicated that 4 out of 10 Americans admit to harboring negative attitudes toward Muslims. Yet, this is likely due to ignorance, for most Americans—according to the same polls—have very little contact with their Muslim neighbors. When Americans get to know their fellow American Muslims, much of the bias disappears.

Have the Islamophobes succeeded in painting Muslims into the box of terror? Has their oft-repeated mantra, "Not all Muslims are terrorists, but all terrorists are Muslim," permeated successfully into the mainstream mindset? Again, perhaps partly. Yet, there may be something else in the background that is contributing to this double standard when it comes to terror.

Looking at the pictures of the 9 men arrested, there is nothing out of the ordinary about them. They are as "ordinary looking" as any other American. I suspect that many Americans may see themselves in the 9 militia members who were arrested and charged. It may be difficult for them to see that these are alleged terrorists because that may mean that anyone, including themselves, has the potential to become so criminal as to plan to bomb a police officer's funeral. It is much easier to see the "other" as being depraved enough to become a terrorist; it is much more difficult to see it in yourself or someone you know.

But the fact remains that anyone—foreign or domestic, Christian or Muslim—can become a terrorist. Terror has no ethnicity or religion, despite what some may say to the contrary. Indeed, Dr. Gary Cass of the Christian Anti-Defamation Commission echoed this sentiment when he said, "Even if they identify themselves as Christians, what they were allegedly planning is absolutely contrary to Christianity. They may have illicitly co-opted the Christian faith to justify their murderous intentions, but it is defamatory for the media to keep referring to them as Christians. They are simply terrorists." Our point exactly. After the arrest of the Hutaree, one would hope more Americans will come to understand the same with Muslims.

> "Americans have far more to fear from
> the Secular Militia than the 'Christian'
> Militia."

The "Secular Militia" Is More Dangerous than Any Christian Militia

Dave Daubenmire

Dave Daubenmire is founder and president of Pass the Salt Ministries and Minutemen United and is affiliated with the Pass the Salt *radio show heard in Columbus, Ohio. In the following viewpoint he argues that the arrest and persecution of the Hutaree fits into a government agenda of undermining the Christian Right. He says that the Hutaree are probably not dangerous. The true danger, he says, comes from leftists who use lies and legal tactics to oppress Christians and destroy the American way. He calls these leftists a secular militia.*

As you read, consider the following questions:

1. Daubenmire says that the Tea Party movement was the first sign of what?
2. According to the author, why can the militia that the

FBI arrested not be Christian if they threatened to kill policemen?

3. What does Daubenmire say is the function of the Southern Poverty Law Center?

Call me Mr. Black Helicopter or try and write me off as a "conspiracy theorist" but something is really fishy about the recent arrest [in March 2010] of the "Christian Militia" in Michigan. I have learned over the years that there is more to most stories than meets the eyes.

People vs. Government

This is just too convenient for me. A few months ago we found out that our Department of Homeland Insecurity had determined that the greatest threat to America weren't the "Hitlers in Headscarves" [referring derogatorily to Muslim extremists] . . . , but Mom and Pop Americans who had the temerity to take their frustrations to the streets. The Tea-Party movement, although clearly spontaneously arising from the heartland, was the first sign of push back from patriotic Americans who were finally realizing that the United States Government was waging war against the freedoms of the United States citizens.

[Secretary of Homeland Security] Janet Napolitano released a report informing her "officers" that those who were showing up at the Tea Parties were the folks who were most threatening to America. Perhaps she was referring to what [President Barack] Obama and his Czars have clearly deduced—the American people are a threat to the American government.

I watched throughout the Cap and Trade fiasco [a plan to regulate carbon emissions to reduce global warming], followed by the August [2010 congressional] recess and the unwillingness of our elected officials to meet with those they represent [about health care reform], the loss of Ted Kennedy's seat in Taxachusetts, the Louisiana Purchase, Cornhusker kickback [a deal alleged to have allowed passage of health care reform in 2010], legislation by the highest bidder, several marches on Washington, to cries of "racism and violence" against those whom Secretary Napolitano had already warned us were the real terrorists.

CNN, Fox News, MSNBC, and the deadstream media were frothing all over each other interviewing "dignitaries" who had been "threatened" and "called names" by the "right wing" Tea Party crowd. *"If someone doesn't do something this whole thing is going to turn violent,"* the talking heads warned us.

FBI Arrests Were Convenient

Well right on cue, our friends at the FBI were able to break up a "right-wing" group of "Christian Militia" who were planning to "kill the police." How convenient that the Feds were on the alert, staging the raid, poisoning public opinion, and proving Janet Napolitano to be a prophet. We all know how violent those Christians are—allowing saliva to fly from their mouths when yelling at legislative larcenists. (Where is [secretary of Health and Human Services] Kathleen Sebelius win [*sic*] we need her? Perhaps she could teach us how not to froth at the mouth when we are angry.) Something smells to me—and it ain't halitosis [bad breath].

I have no idea who this "Christian" Militia is, but are they inferring that the "Christian" Militia is more dangerous than, say, the "Muslim" Militia?" I suppose Major [Nidal Malik] Hasan at Ft. Hood [who in 2009, went on a shooting spree on base] wasn't part of any militia—just a good man bullied into violence. I guess actually killing soldiers is not nearly as bad as "threatening" to kill policemen. Just curious, have any of the members of Major Hasan's militia been arrested?

Let's be clear. Christians don't kill cops. If this "militia" threatened to do so then they are not Christians. . . .

Just what is a "Christian Militia"? According to the dictionary a militia is *"a body of citizen soldiers as distinguished from professional soldiers."* What distinguishes a "Christian" militia from an "atheistic" militia, or a "patriot" militia, or better yet, a "state" militia? Would Secretary Napolitano speak the same way about the "Islamic" Militia carousing around the globe? Are we now to assume that this group arrested in Michigan is representative of all "Christians"? Would we get away with calling the gangs trolling our inner cities a "black" militia? (I smell [black civil rights activist] Al Sharpton . . . er . . . a rat.) Somebody is being set up.

The Secular Militia

Call me paranoid, but I don't like the direction this whole thing is heading. I think we have a lot more to fear from the Secular Militia who are destroying the soul of this nation. There is a civil war going on in this country, for sure. It is a war where Christianity is the enemy and words are the grenades. The Secular Militia are very well organized, fully financed, and embedded in every area of our society. Permit me to point them out to you.

One branch of the secular militia is the Southern Poverty Law Center Militia. The SPLC is the platoon in charge of determining what speech is protected and what speech is hateful.

The American Civil Liberties Union Militia is the legal arm of the Secular Militia. They are charged with tearing down any semblance of Christianity in America by threatening those who publicly practice it.

The National Education Association Militia is the educational branch of the Secular Militia who are following orders to rewrite the history of America, destroying the generational bond that ties families together.

The NAACP [National Association for the Advancement of Colored People] Militia is the racist SWAT team charged with digging trenches between Americans into which we all are eventually pushed.

Planned Parenthood Militia is the population police charged

Failures to Confront Islamic Extremism

DoD [the Department of Defense] possessed compelling evidence that [Nidal Malik] Hasan [who went on a shooting spree at Ft. Hood in 2009] embraced [Islamic] views so extreme that it should have disciplined him or discharged him from the military, but DoD failed to take action against him. Indeed, a number of policies on commanders' authority, extremism, and personnel gave supervisors in his chain of command the authority to take such actions. It is clear from this failure that DoD lacks the institutional culture, through updated policies and training, sufficient to inform commanders and all levels of servicemembers how to identify radicalization to violent Islamist extremism and to distinguish this ideology from the peaceful practice of Islam.

To address this failure, the Department of Defense should confront the threat of radicalization to violent Islamist extremism among servicemembers explicitly and directly and strengthen associated policies and training.

Joseph I. Lieberman and Susan Collins, US Senate Committee on Homeland Security and Governmental Affairs, February 5, 2011.

with keeping enlistments of certain people groups to a minimum, while lining the pockets of those who love death.

The National Council of Churches Militia is the special ops charged with infiltrating the seminaries of America and destroying the minds of the Christian leadership convincing them that God was the ultimate homophobe.

The Mainstream Media Militia is the Tokyo Rose [World War

II Japanese radio propagandist] of the Secular Militia, charged with undermining every foundation upon which this nation was built and convincing us that clinging to our God and our Guns was old-fashioned and out of style.

Hollywood and the Screen Actors Guild Militia is a group of "don't ask don't tell" soldiers charged with undermining the morals of American children by changing the monogamous relationship into a sexual smorgasbord.

The National Bar Association Militia has assumed the duty of weakening Americans through the terrorism of "civil rights" lawsuits aimed at silencing the freedom of speech.

The Internal Revenue Service Militia is like the paratroopers that parachute in behind enemy lines to abscond with the allies' resources and clamping a chain on churches who speak the Truth.

The National Organization For Women Militia are the WAC's [Women's Army Corps] of the Secular Media charged with castration of the American male and the liberation of lion-like lesbians.

The GLSEN [Gay, Lesbian and Straight Education Network] Militia has been given the mission of weakening this nation by blurring all gender roles and sexual morality and homosexualizing GI Joe.

At War for the Nation

I could go on.

We are at war for this nation. It is a battle between those who fear the Lord and those who do not; Between those who believe Jesus is Lord and those who do not; Between those who think we work for the government and those who think the government should work for us.

It is clear that secular government has a militia and that they are determined to do all they can to squash the Christians. The war has already been declared. They aren't fighting it with guns but with lies and intimidation.

And fear not them which kill the body, but are not able to kill the soul: but rather fear him which is able to destroy both soul and body in hell. Matt. 10:28

Americans have far more to fear from the Secular Militia than the "Christian" Militia. They are destroying this nation . . . one grenade at a time.

Periodical and Internet Sources Bibliography

The following articles have been selected to supplement the diverse views presented in this chapter.

Junaid Afeef	"Hutaree Militia—Right Wing Extremists—Targeting American Muslims," *American Muslim Journal*, March 29, 2010. http://americanmuslimjournal.typepad.com.
Anti-Defamation League	"Christian Identity," 2005. www.adl.org.
Billy Atwell	"The Hutaree 'Christian Militia': Hardly Christian," *For the Greater Glory* (blog), April 1, 2010. www.billyatwell.org.
Chip Berlet	"'Christian Warrior': Who Are the Hutaree Militia and Where Did They Come From?," Religion Dispatches, March 31, 2010. www.religiondispatches.org.
Frederick Clarkson	"The Faith-Based Militia: When Is Terrorism 'Christian?'," Religion Dispatches, April 8, 2010. www.religiondispatches.org.
Classic Liberal (blog)	"No Matter What, Hutaree Raids Will Be Spun Against Christians," March 29, 2010. http://the-classic-liberal.com.
Yasmin Mogahed	"Does the Hutaree Militia Represent Christianity? A Muslim Knows Better," *Huffington Post*, March 31, 2010. www.huffingtonpost.com.

For Further Discussion

Chapter 1

1. Do either Abraham H. Foxman or Larry Keller link any specific violent acts to the militia movement since its resurgence in 2008? If so, what acts are they, and do those acts suggest that militias should be monitored by the government, as Eileen Pollack suggests? Why or why not?

2. Bruce McQuain argues that the rise of militias in the '90s led to "not much of anything." Is that true, do you think? Explain your answer.

Chapter 2

1. Robert H. Churchill's viewpoint argues that libertarian ideas have inspired the militia movement. Does that suggest that the government should collect information on people espousing libertarian ideas? Why or why not? Consider and cite from Steve Newton's viewpoint in your answer.

2. Does Kurt Hofmann renounce violence against the government in his viewpoint? Does Hofmann refute or confirm Dennis Henigan's argument that militias and the NRA are providing a constitutional justification for violence? Explain your answer, citing from the viewpoints.

Chapter 3

1. Supreme Court justice Antonin Scalia is often associated with originalism—the idea that the Constitution should be interpreted according to its original intent. What does Saul Cornell say the original intent of the Second Amendment was? Would following the original intent as stated by Cornell make sense in today's society? Why or why not?

2. What arguments does the Army National Guard use to bolster its claim that the organizatin is heir to the militia

discussed in the Constitution? Would the Army National Guard object to the state militias discussed by James Carafano and Jessica Zuckerman? Explain your answer.

Chapter 4

1. Based on the viewpoints in this chapter, do you think it is fair to characterize some militias as "Christian militias"? Why or why not?

2. Dave Daubenmire argues that the real danger to the United States comes not from Christian militias but from "the secular militia." Does Daubenmire convince you that a militia like the Hutaree is equivalent to an organization like the Southern Poverty Law Center? Explain your answer.

Organizations to Contact

The editors have compiled the following list of organizations concerned with the issues debated in this book. The descriptions are derived from materials provided by the organizations. All have publications or information available for interested readers. The list was compiled on the date of publication of the present volume; names, addresses, phone and fax numbers, and e-mail and Internet addresses may change. Be aware that many organizations take several weeks or longer to respond to inquiries, so allow as much time as possible.

Anti-Defamation League (ADL)

823 United Nations Plaza
New York, NY 10017
(212) 490-2525 • fax: (212) 867-0779
website: www.adl.org

ADL works to stop the defamation of Jews and to ensure fair treatment for all US citizens. It advocates state and federal governments' adoption of penalty-enhancement (hate crime) laws and antiparamilitary training statutes as a means to fight hate crimes. Its website includes news reports, fact sheets, profiles, and reports such as "The Militia Movement—Extremism in America."

Brady Center to Prevent Gun Violence

1225 Eye Street NW, Suite 1100
Washington, DC 20005
(202) 898-0792 • fax: (202) 371-9615
website: www.bradynetwork.org

The Brady Center is committed to creating an America free from gun violence. It works to pass and enforce sensible federal and state gun regulations through activism, increasing public awareness, and working to elect public officials who support sensible gun laws. The group's website includes fact sheets, blogs, news releases, and other information.

Cato Institute

1000 Massachusetts Ave. NW
Washington, DC 20001-5403
(202) 842-0200 • fax: (202) 842-3490
website: www.cato.org

The Cato Institute is a nonprofit, public policy research organization promoting the principles of libertarianism. It analyzes all aspects of the US government's domestic and foreign policy, offers recommendations to policy makers, and educates the public on current issues debated in the government. The Cato Institute in general supports the right to bear arms, opposes gun regulation, and opposes surveillance and prosecution of militia members. Its website includes reports, book chapters, blogs, news updates, and more, including essays such as "The 'Militia Panic' of 2009" and "Gun Control on Trial: Inside the Supreme Court Battle over the Second Amendment."

Militia of Montana (MOM)

PO Box 1486
Noxon, MT 59853
(406) 847-2735
e-mail: militia@montana.com
website: www.militiaofmontana.com

MOM is an organized paramilitary organization. It works to inform the public of threats and trains members in military preparedness in case of emergency. Its website includes online catalogs, special reports, and other information.

National Guard

1411 Jefferson Davis Highway
Arlington, VA 22202-3231
(703) 607-2584

e-mail: oncall.pao@ng.army.mil
website: www.ng.mil

The National Guard is a reserve military force composed of citizen soldiers. National Guard members may be mobilized to serve in active army duty and may also be called up by state governors to respond to domestic emergencies such as hurricanes or floods. The National Guard website includes news briefings, archived copies of the now-defunct National Guard newspaper *OnGuard*, archived copies of *Foundations Magazine*, and reports and essays.

National Rifle Association (NRA)
11250 Waples Mill Road
Fairfax, VA 22030
(800) 672-3888
website: home.nra.org

The NRA is a nonprofit organization that advocates for the protection of gun rights and promotion of firearm ownership. It advocates for legislation at the federal and state levels and sponsors firearm safety training courses. Its website includes blogs, news notices, ratings of the gun rights records of candidates, and pages about legislation, guns and hunting, and other topics of interest to members. It also publishes several magazines, such as *American Rifleman* and *Shooting Illustrated*.

Oklahoma City National Memorial and Museum
620 N. Harvey Ave.
Oklahoma City, OK 73102
(405) 235-3313; toll-free: (888) 542-4673
website: www.oklahomacitynationalmemorial.org

The Oklahoma City National Memorial and Museum is dedicated to the memory of those killed in the Oklahoma City bombing of 1995. The museum plans and holds exhibits and provides information to the public about the events of the bombing and its aftermath. The website includes information about current exhibits and educational and historical materials.

Southeast Michigan Volunteer Militia

7578 Mission Road
Alanson, MI 49706
(616) 548-5878 • fax: (616) 548-4867
e-mail: nolso@sunny.ncmc.cc.mi.us
website: www.michiganmilitia.com/SMVM/smvm.htm

The Southeast Michigan Volunteer Militia is a paramilitary organization dedicated to defending the Constitution of the United States and the Constitution of Michigan. It trains members in survival skills and works to educate and inform the public, as well as sponsoring an annual public shooting event. Its website includes reports on the group's activities, answers to frequently asked questions, and other information. It also publishes *Militia*, a bimonthly newsletter.

Southern Poverty Law Center (SPLC)

PO Box 2087
Montgomery AL 36102
(334) 264-0286 • fax: (334) 264-8891

The Southern Poverty Law Center litigates civil cases to protect the rights of poor people, particularly when those rights are threatened by white supremacist groups. The affiliated Klanwatch Project and Militia Task Force collect data on white supremacist groups and militias and promote the adoption and enforcement of antiparamilitary training laws. The SPLC website includes numerous publications and reports, including "Active 'Patriot' Groups in the United States in 2010" and "Ku Klux Klan: A History of Racism."

Supreme Court of the United States

1 First Street NE
Washington, DC 20543

(202) 479-3000

website: www.supremecourt.gov

The Supreme Court of the United States is the highest court in the country. Its website includes the Supreme Court *Journal*, which contains the official minutes of Supreme Court deliberations. The site also includes recent court decisions and opinions, including those that deal with Second Amendment issues and gun rights.

Bibliography of Books

Dick Armey and Matt Kibbe

Give Us Liberty: A Tea Party Manifesto. New York: HarperCollins, 2010.

Michael Barkun

Religion and the Racist Right: The Origins of the Christian Identity Movement. Chapel Hill: University of North Carolina Press, 1997.

Peter Brown and Daniel Abel

Outgunned: Up Against the NRA—the First Complete Insider Account of the Battle over Gun Control. New York: Free Press, 2002.

Patrick J. Charles

The Second Amendment: The Intent and Its Interpretation by the States and the Supreme Court. Jefferson, NC: McFarland, 2009.

Brian Doherty

Gun Control on Trial: Inside the Supreme Court Battle over the Second Amendment. Washington, DC: Cato Institute, 2008.

Brian Doherty

Radicals for Capitalism: A Freewheeling History of the Modern American Libertarian Movement. New York: Public Affairs, 2008.

Richard Feldman	*Ricochet: Confessions of a Gun Lobbyist*. Hoboken, NJ: Wiley, 2008.
John George and Laird M. Wilcox	*American Extremists: Militias, Supremacists, Klansmen, Communists, and Others*. Amherst, NY: Prometheus Books, 1996.
Kristin A. Goss	*Disarmed: The Missing Movement for Gun Control in America*. Princeton, NJ: Princeton University Press, 2006.
Stephen P. Halbrook	*The Founders' Second Amendment: Origins of the Right to Bear Arms*. Chicago: Ivan R. Dee, 2008.
William E. Hudson	*The Libertarian Illusion: Ideology, Public Policy, and the Assault on the Common Good*. Washington, DC: CQ Press, 2008.
Mark Juergensmeyer	*Global Rebellion: Religious Challenges to the Secular State, from Christian Militias to Al Qaeda*. Berkeley: University of California Press, 2009.
Alan Korwin and David B. Kopel	*The* Heller *Case: Gun Rights Affirmed*. Scottsdale, AZ: Bloomfield Press, 2008.

Wayne LaPierre — *The Essential Second Amendment Guide.* 2nd ed. Los Angeles: WND Books, 2009.

Jill Lepore — *The Whites of Their Eyes: The Tea Party's Revolution and the Battle over American History.* Princeton, NJ: Princeton University Press, 2010.

Daniel Levitas — *The Terrorist Next Door: The Militia Movement and the Radical Right.* New York: St. Martin's, 2002.

Edward T. Linenthal — *The Unfinished Bombing: Oklahoma City in American Memory.* New York: Oxford University Press, 2001.

John R. Lott Jr. — *More Guns, Less Crime: Understanding Crime and Gun Control Laws.* 3rd ed. Chicago: University of Chicago Press, 2010.

Eric Mann — *Katrina's Legacy: White Racism and Black Reconstruction in New Orleans and the Gulf Coast.* Los Angeles: Frontlines Press, 2006.

Darren Mulloy — *American Extremism: History, Politics, and the Militia Movement.* New York: Routledge, 2004.

Barry M. Stentiford

The American Home Guard: The State Militia in the Twentieth Century. College Station: Texas A&M University Press, 2002.

Stuart A. Wright

Patriots, Politics, and the Oklahoma City Bombing. New York: Cambridge University Press, 2007.

Kate Zernike

Boiling Mad: Inside Tea Party America. New York: Times Books, 2010.

Leonard Zeskind

Blood and Politics: The History of the White Nationalist Movement from the Margins to the Mainstream. New York: Farrar, Straus & Giroux, 2009.

Index